THE WEST TENNESSEE HISTORICAL SOCIETY: GUIDE TO ARCHIVES AND COLLECTIONS

Eleanor McKay, editor

Manuscripts processed by Robert D. Bohanan,
with assistance from Hans Ryan and Ann Washington

Memphis, TN: Mississippi Valley Collection and
Memphis State University Press, 1979

Copyright © 1979 by
Memphis State University Press

Funded by grants from the West Tennessee Historical Society and from the National Historical Records and Publications Commission

All rights reserved. No part of this book may be reproduced or utilized in any form or by any means, electronic or mechanical, including photocopying and recording, or by any information storage and retrieval system, without permission from the publisher.

Manufactured in the
United States of America
ISBN 0-87870-050-1

Table of Contents

Introduction
1. Archives and Manuscripts 9
2. Books 22
3. Photographs and Images 28
4. Periodicals 33
5. Maps 36
6. Artifacts 38
7. Vertical File 42
8. Sheet Music 45
9. Tape Recordings 48
10. Memphis Bicentennial Commission 49
11. Back Inventory 50
Index 53

INTRODUCTION

THE WEST TENNESSEE HISTORICAL SOCIETY—
A SHORT HISTORY

The West Tennessee Historical Society, Inc., traces its history to 1857 and is the descendent of four predecessor organizations in the western Grand Division of Tennessee. That year the Old Folks of Shelby County met monthly and published a monthly journal, *Old Folks Record*, from which J. D. Davis derived much information for his *History of Memphis* (Memphis, 1873). In 1866 the Old Folks' historical role was taken over by the Confederate Relief and Historical Association of Memphis, which was re-organized in 1869 as the Confederate Historical Association and in 1884 as Camp 28, United Confederate Veterans. Its historian, Captain J. Harvey Mathes, wrote *The Old Guard In Grey* (Memphis, 1889). Judge John Preston Young, a leader in the Confederate Historical Association, organized the Memphis Historical Society around the turn of the century. In 1935 the Society changed its name to the West Tennessee Historical Society, electing Dr. Marshall Wingfield its first president.

On 28 September 1950 the West Tennessee Historical Society gave way to the West Tennessee Historical Society, Inc., incorporated in Shelby County. The incorporators took over the affairs of the unincorporated society and granted membership to members in good standing of the predecessor organization as of September 1, 1950. Presidents of the society have included:

   Marshall Wingfield, 1938-1961
   John Henry Davis, 1962-1963
   Charles E. Pool, 1964
   Buford C. Utley, 1965-1967
   James E. Roper, 1968-1971
   Charles A. Bobbitt, 1971-1976
   Charles W. Crawford, 1976-

The membership, about 500 in 1978, draws from the West Tennessee counties of Benton, Carroll, Chester, Crockett, Decatur, Dyer, Fayette, Gibson, Hardeman, Hardin, Haywood, Henderson, Henry, Lake, Lauderdale, Madison, McNairy, Obion, Shelby, Tipton, and Weakley.

West Tennessee Historical Society members are invited to meetings held usually in Memphis at the Memphis Pink Palace Museum every month between September and May, except for a spring and a fall outing at historical sites elsewhere in the Grand Division. These meetings feature the reading of a scholarly paper or the presentation of an audio visual show about some aspect of West Tennessee history. Members also receive a copy of the *Papers*, published in the fall. In 1978 the membership dues are $8.00 for regular members and $10.00 for sustaining members, both payable annually.

Life members make one payment of $100, which frees them of further dues. Those wishing only to subscribe to the *Papers* pay $5.00 per year.

The Society governs itself through the annual election of a president, a vice-president for Shelby County, a vice-president for the remainder of West Tennessee, a vice-president at large, a recording secretary, a corresponding secretary, a treasurer, and an assistant treasurer. In recent years, the Curator of the Society has been the Curator of the Mississippi Valley Collection at Memphis State University, where the West Tennessee Historical Society's archives and collections have resided since 1974. The president also appoints five members from throughout the Grand Division to the Executive Board. These officers of the Society meet at least quarterly to make policy decisions and to conduct necessary business. They appoint the editor and several associate editors for the West Tennessee Historical Society *Papers*, an annual volume that began publication in 1947 to disseminate scholarly papers and critical reviews of materials concerning the history of West Tennessee. Members of the editorial and executive boards must be members of the Society. Members may also serve on the membership committee or the hospitality committee, both of which function at every meeting of the society.

THE PROVENANCE OF THE COLLECTION

In 1974 the West Tennessee Historical Society accepted the offer of Dr. Billy M. Jones, President of Memphis State University, to locate the society's archives and collections permanently in the Mississippi Valley Collection of the Memphis State University Libraries. The society had stored its material at the Memphis Pink Palace Museum since the late 1940s, and before that, various officers of the society had stored portions of the collection at their homes or offices. Lacking a permanent home for its holdings, the Society was unable to maintain an adequate record of what it owned or of new acquisitions by the society. This resulted in a gradually weakened collecting program and in poor donor relations over the years.

Now, however, with the publication of this guide. the Society will begin to build its collections again. Persons knowing of the location of suitable material or those holding materials once a part of the society's collections are asked to contact the president of the West Tennessee Historical Society, who can be reached at Box 82260, Memphis State University, Memphis, TN., 38152.

The collection is available for research use by members of the historical society or by qualified researchers in the reading room of the Mississippi Valley Collection of the Memphis State University Libraries. The reading room is generally open 8 a.m. to 9 p.m. on Mondays and 8 a.m. to 5 p.m. Tuesday through Friday, although the evening hours may vary according to the university's schedule.

THE FUTURE OF THE COLLECTION

Much documentation about the history of West Tennessee must still be acquired if researchers are to prepare comprehensive studies of this Grand

Division of the State of Tennessee. Personal papers, the records of organizations and businesses, ephemeral material, and photographs concerning West Tennessee need to be added to the WTHS's collections, where they can be processed and made accessible for research use. Any person willing to donate such material or knowing of the location of such material should contact:

    The Curator
    West Tennessee Historical Society
    Mississippi Valley Collection
    Memphis State University
    Memphis, TN 38152

THE COLLECTION—GUIDE ENTRIES

There are twelve categories of holdings of the West Tennessee Historical Society, including the archives of the society, manuscripts, books, photographs, periodicals, maps, artifacts, a vertical file of ephemera, sheet music, tape recordings, souvenir material from the Memphis Bicentennial Commission, and the society's inventory of its *Papers*, books, and pamphlets. All the society's holdings are now processed and accessible through this guide. None of this material is restricted. For ease of storage and retrieval, the manuscript collections, including material of varying media, have been broken down and arranged according to these categories. For each manuscript collection, there is a descriptive register on file in the Mississippi Valley Collection reading room; the separation sheet to that register contains descriptions of all separated material with a note concerning its location. Researchers should consult the index to this guide for a comprehensive overview by proper name or important subject headings of the WTHS's holdings except for the books and sheet music. They are indexed only by author and title. Index terms have been suggested by the collections themselves. Researchers primarily interested in the types of collections held by the society should first consult the guide entries for each media category; each list is alphabetically arranged by collection title, and the entries are numbered sequentially within each category.

This guide is partially funded by grants from the West Tennessee Historical Society and from the National Historical and Publications Commission.

ARCHIVES AND MANUSCRIPTS

AM 1. **ARCHIVES**
West Tennessee Historical Society, Inc. Archives, 1922—(1947-1978). 4 containers totalling 3.3 cu. ft.

Correspondence, minutes, unpublished articles, reports, newletters, clippings, membership lists, agendas, and other business and financial records of the historical society serving the western Grand Division of Tennessee. Although the Society traces its history back to 1857, the bulk of the records, 1922—(1947-1978), do not document any of the predecessor organizations except the West Tennessee Historical Society, which the West Tennessee Historical Society, Inc. succeeded in 1950. Arranged chronologically and thereunder by subject, the files reveal the Historical Society's activities regarding publications, especially of the annual *Papers*; meetings; historical markers; unpublished papers of local historical interest; reference questions from the general public; correspondence; and general financial and business papers (some oversized) detailing the normal operations of the Society. Significant correspondents include influential members of the Society, especially Buford C. Utley and Marshall Wingfield. Transferred by the West Tennessee Historical Society to the Mississippi Valley Collection, Memphis State University, in 1974.

MANUSCRIPT COLLECTIONS:

AM 2. *Adamson, C. B., Dispatches, 1864.* 1 container, totalling .3 cu. ft.
Manuscript copies of Confederate dispatches received at the C. B. Adamson drug store in Jackson, TN in 1864, and xerox copies of the more fragile dispatches. These dispatches reflect the kind of news received at home from the battle front, and how it was disseminated from the trading and agricultural center of Jackson to the rest of West Tennessee and other points in the Confederacy. Most of these dispatches were sent by two reporters, Jack Stephens and Jno. B. Morris from all points in the Confederacy, including Richmond; they were transmitted mainly via Corinth and Tupelo, MS. There are fourteen pages of copies of dispatches sent by General Robert E. Lee. Donated by Mrs. Annie Lee Applegate, Memphis, in 1955; Mrs. Applegate was the granddaughter of Dr. Adamson.

AM 3. *Bennett, Ella Costillo* (1865-1932). *Papers,* 1859-1947. 2 containers totalling 2 cubic feet.
Papers, 1865-1947, of Ella Costillo Bennett, a journalist and author,

including a review of a speech on the Civil War by William G. Brownlaw, 1866-1870; her manuscript published in 1915 concerning a black minister's sermon in "Darktown"; two play manuscripts, 1920?, n.d.; a scrapbook, c. 1930, containing several photographs of her, and typescript and manuscript copies of her poems on such themes as love, patriotism, and religion. Another scrapbook, c. 1947, maintained and annotated by her sister, Mary L. Nichols, (1856-1947) of Walsenburg, Colorado, preserves an extremely detailed family history of the Costillos and Nichols in Memphis, TN. It also provides extensive information on the lifestyle and declining standard of living of wealthy slaveholders before, during, and after the Civil War, and on the lack of educational facilities for children in Memphis in the 1850's despite the thriving economy of this waterfront city. She included photographs of beaten slaves, regimental doctors during the Civil War, Mary Todd Lincoln and her son Robert Lincoln, black leader Frederick Douglass, abolitionists Henry Ward Beecher and John Brown, and the 1906 San Francisco earthquake. Other topics documented in the Nichols scrapbook include changes in the economy of Denver, Colorado during the late 19th century when Chinese immigrants replaced blacks at menial jobs; the silver mining boom towns of the Southwest and the 1894 Coxey's March of unemployed miners on Washington, D.C.; and the fear of a labor war in the Southwest in the late 19th century. Many pages are decorated with elaborately colored and decorated greeting cards, cut-outs, or doilies. Numerous photographs, artifacts, and periodicals were placed in other parts of the West Tennessee Historical Society holdings. Donated by Mary L. Bennett, Los Angeles, California, n.d.

AM 4. *Donaldson, R. C.* (1877-1961). *Papers,* 1934-1960. 6 containers totalling 3.3 cu. ft.
Correspondence, diaries, historical writings, archeological reports, and scrapbooks, 1934-1960, of a prominent Lake County, TN banker, lawyer, and amateur archeologist. One series contains his research materials and reports on West Tennessee during the Civil War and on its archeological sites, especially at the T. O. Fuller site in Shelby County. Other series include loose clippings concerning the history of West Tennessee and the lower Mississippi Valley; Donaldson's diaries, 1934, 1938-1960, concerning his activities as a lawyer, banker, collector, and historian in the small town of Tiptonville; and nine scrapbooks of mainly local newspaper clippings on the history of West Tennessee. The scrapbooks contain copies of his column, "Lake County Bygones" from the *Lake County Banner*; a typescript copy of the 1856 diary of C. M. Peacock of Tiptonville; extensive clippings on the 1937 flood of the Mississippi River; and clippings concerning his 1958 discovery of the 1858 diary of Margaret Q. C. Griffis. The diary is also reprinted. Provenance unknown.

AM 5. *Gordon, George W.* (1836-1911). *Papers.* 1863-1912. 1 container, totalling 3 cu. ft.

Papers, 1863-1912, unevenly documenting the career of the Confederate Brigadier General, lawyer, politician, Congressman, and first Imperial Klansman of the Ku Klux Klan. They include his one-page, handwritten account of the Battle of Chickamauga, 1863; a copy of the 1863 state statute and commission, appointing him a commissioner of the State of Missouri empowered to take depositions and fulfill other legal duties for Missouri while residing in Memphis; his scrapbook, 1904-1905, containing orders, clippings, correspondence, news releases, membership attendance lists, and other items concerning his command of the Tennessee Division of the United Confederate Veterans; and memorial addresses following his death, 1912; n.d. Donated to the West Tennessee Historical Society by Mrs. Alma Ramsey Bowers, Memphis, 1 Jan 1957.

AM 6. *Hamner, James H. (1840?-after 1918) - Stacy, Mrs. C. M. Correspondence*, 1861-1865. 1 container, totalling 3 cu. ft.

Letters between a mother, Mrs. Caledonia Musadora Scales Hamner Stacy of West Point, MS and her son, Captain James H. Hamner (CSA), of Memphis, 1861-1865, with a typed short history and slightly edited transcript of the letters by his daughter Laura V. Hamner of Amarillo, Texas. Mrs. Stacy's letters, the bulk of the collection, detail the hardships she endured on the home front while dying of tuberculosis, managing the slaves, and fearing the Union occupation troops. Hamner rose to the rank of Captain while serving the South under General Nathan Bedford Forrest. He was wounded in a battle at Fort Donelson, TN, and served as an ordnance officer through the remainder of the war. His letters describe his life in the army, give details of the battles in which he saw action (including Franklin, Murfreesboro, and Chickamauga), and discuss his duties as an ordnance officer. Provenance unknown.

AM 7. *Johnson, Robert* (1915-1973). *Clippings*, 1962-1973. 3 containers, totalling 3 cu. ft.

Tearsheets, from the *Memphis Press-Scimitar*, 1962-1973, including Johnson's daily human interest column, "Good Evening". They are arranged chronologically, and only lack the columns for 1963-1964. Compiled after his death and donated to the West Tennessee Historical Society by his widow, Marie Sargent Morris Johnson, Memphis, spring 1974.

AM 8. *Memphis and Charleston Railroad Depot* (Memphis, TN) *Controversy. Records*, 1964-1968. 1 container, totalling 3 cu. ft.

Four folders of correspondence, clippings, histories of the depot, reports, minutes of meetings, petitions, photographs, maps, and press releases, 1964-1968, documenting the history of the oldest railroad depot in continuous use in the United States, and the unsuccessful efforts of Memphis organizations to save it from destruction. The depot was constructed in Memphis at Adams and Lauderdale streets in 1854 by the Memphis and Charleston Railroad, and later changed its name to the Southern Railroad Depot following the sale of the Memphis and Charleston Railroad. The depot figured prominently in the Civil War Battle of Memphis. The organizations trying to save the depot from the Memphis Housing Authority's urban renewal plan included the Citizens Advisory Committee, Association for the Preservation of Tennessee Antiquities, West Tennessee Historical Society, Shelby County Historical Commission, the Downtown Auxiliary Unit of the Model Railroaders, Good Earth Garden Club, and Memphis branches of the Sons of Confederate Veterans and Colonial Dames of America. Although they were unable to prevent the destruction of the depot in 1968, the combined work of the groups did result in the 1967 formation of the Memphis Landmarks Commission by the City of Memphis. Provenance unknown.

AM 9. *Meriwether Family. Papers*, 1751-1951. 2 containers totalling 2 cu. ft. Papers, 1751-1952, of the Meriwether Family arranged in four series; includes correspondence, diaries, legal papers, literary and political writings, scrapbooks, and other materials. Family members documented include Minor Lee Meriwether (1827-1910), his wife Elizabeth Avery Meriwether (1824-1917), and their children Avery (1857-1883), Rivers Blythe (1859-1896), and Minor Lee Meriwether (1862-1966), who resided in Memphis, TN, and St. Louis, MO. Minor and Elizabeth Avery Meriwether's correspondence reflects their strong commitment to freedom for all, including blacks and women; they both attended the National Suffragist Convention in 1879. Included are letters of Minor's father, Garrett Minor (1794-1851), of Cabin Row, Kentucky, to relatives in Virginia describing life in the region. There are also papers of other members of the Meriwether, Minor, Brockman, and Douglas Families. The series includes letters among various family members living in Tennessee, Kentucky, and Virginia. Other significant letters to Minor and Elizabeth Avery Meriwether include eleven letters of Jefferson and Varina Davis writing about their social, philanthropic, and personal lives, 1872-1886. Subjects include the death of their son Joseph E. Davis in the arms of Minor Meriwether, and two letters, 1884, 1886, of Senator L. Q. C. Lamar of Mississippi responding to their constituent mail. There is also an 1875 letter from Minor Meriwether to Nathan Bedford Forrest describing a dispute they had. The correspondence of Elizabeth Avery Meriwether, and of others in the series of Meriwether Family Papers, reveals much about the life and career of this suffargist leader. The bulk of the correspondence was originally bound in a volume and annotated by Minor Meriwether. In the series of Meriwether Family Papers are legal documents such as wills, deeds, and tax receipts of the family, c. 1772-1874, as well as documents concerning Minor's political activity in Memphis, Shelby County, and statewide, 1868-1875; obituaries on Avery Meriwether, 1883; two manuscripts by Elizabeth Avery Meriwether. "The Ku Klux Klan" (1877) and "Black and White" (1883); two manuscripts by her son Avery, "English Tyranny and Irish Suffering" (1881) and "A Chapter in the History of Vivum—Ovo" (1882); and an allegory on free trade attributed to Edgar Allen Poe, and reprinted from Avery and Lee's newspaper *The Free Trader*. The series of papers of Lee Meriwether (1862-1966) includes copies of his articles and speeches. They include a speech on Jefferson Davis he gave to a meeting of the United Sons of Confederate Veterans in 1908 and virulent attacks on the New Deal, 1936. There is also a typescript of his diaries, 1884-1910 concerning his extensive travels, government work, and family life. The final series of bound volumes contains the annotated scrapbooks of Minor and Elizabeth Avery Meriwether, and a typescript of her memoirs, *Recollections of 92 Years*; the original diaries, 1894-1910, of their son Lee; and an original 1877 docket of Shelby County, TN's Chancery Court. Donated by Lee Meriwether, St. Louis, Mo, 1960.

AM 10. **MISCELLANEOUS MANUSCRIPTS.**
These are collections ranging in size from one item to one folder. For convenience, they are listed together in the following short entries, but each is fully indexed. Provenance unknown unless mentioned in an entry; the E. B. Ramsey Family of Memphis probably donated the scrapbooks described in entries AM 10:36-46

AM 10: 1. Printed poem, "Lines on the Back of a Confederate Note," n.d., by Major Samuel Alroy Jones extolling patriotism of those loyal to the Confederacy during and since the war despite all hardships. Mounted with $100 Confederate note, dated 1 September 1862. Donated by Alma Ramsey Bowers, Memphis, 1 Jan 1957.

AM 10: 2. Photostatic copy of handwritten letter, 14 October 1833, from Stephen Haynes of Franklin, TN, to his brother Richard Haynes of Union County, Indiana, instructing him to apply for a pension for his Revolutionary War service. Original at the National Archives, Records of the Veterans Administration.

AM 10: 3. Photographic copies of surveyors records, deeds, indentures, and bills of sale concerning land and slaves registered in Weakly County, Tennessee, 1784-1832; includes property owned by David Crockett, Andrew Jackson, Alfred Gardner, John Almus Gardner, David Allison, and George Patton.

AM 10: 4. Xerox Copy of manuscript narrative of Mrs. Agnes Blackwell of Mason Depot, Tipton County, TN, concerning details of her daily life, and her reactions to the news about the war she received travelling as a nurse with Confederate forces of General Earl Van Dorn throughout Mississippi. Although dated 1894, her original account covers the period 11 August - 6 December 1864; perhaps 1894 is the date of the manuscript copy this xerox was made from. Separated from the Marshall Wingfield Manuscripts (See AM 13).

AM 10: 5. Mimeographed copy of typed transcript of the memoirs of Brigadier General William Montgomery Gardner (CSA) telling of his life from childhood through the end of the Civil War. The memoirs were edited from his diary and letters by his daughter Elizabeth McKinne Gardner, and published in *The Commercial Appeal* beginning 30 June 1912. Donated by R. P. Richardson, Memphis, TN, 16 May 1960.

AM 10: 6. Notebook, 1863, of Captain D. H. Todd, 21st Louisiana Volunteers, CSA; includes his brief diary, rosters of his company, pencilled drawings, poems, copies of letters to his superior officers, lists of effects of deceased persons sold at auction, and an account of groceries purchased for the Confederate Army. Separated from the Marshall Wingfield Manuscripts (see AM 13).

AM 10: 7. Positive photostatic copy of extra edition of *Nashville Union*, 15 April 1865, concerning assassination of President Abraham Lincoln.

AM 10: 8. Letter, 13 June 1876, of C. D. McLean of Rossville, Fayette County, TN, to W. T. Avery concerning the early history of Memphis and Shelby County.

AM 10: 9. Papers concerning Dr. John Allen Wyeth, who was born in North Alabama in 1845, served with the Confederacy, and founded the Polyclinic Medical School and Hospital in New York City during the 1880's. The papers include an undated, typed, biographical sketch prepared by John J. Morrow, Jr., of Batesville, Alabama; an undated negative photostat of a social action handbill involving the Polyclinic Hospital's ambulance service; and negative photostats of four letters of Dr. Wyeth, 1909-1921. Separated from the Marshall Wingfield Manuscripts (see AM 13).

AM 10:10 Two full sheets of 1878 U. S. Internal Revenue stamps, one engraved with a portrait of Andrew Jackson, the other with that of Zachary Taylor. Donated by F. W. Lunan, Billerica, Massachusetts, 12 December 1954.

AM 10:11. Four promissory notes for $250.00 each of M. C. Priddy of Memphis to himself, to be paid over an 18-month period following 1 April 1870. Each bears a 15¢ U.S. Internal Revenue stamp.

AM 10:12. Positive photostat of petition, 1864, of trustees of Second Presbyterian Church of Memphis asking that their church building, confiscated by General William T. Sherman, be returned to the congregation for religious use; with reply, 4 March 1864, of President Abraham Lincoln, that the U.S. military "must not undertake to run the church" but only occupy church buildings for the duration of wartime emergencies; and order, 18 March 1864, of Major General S. A. Hurlburt (USA) that the church be returned once the trustees give proof of their loyalty to the union.

AM 10:13. Positive photostat of invitation to attend a Presidential dinner on 14 March 1795, dated 6 March 1795, and addressed to Jno. Shoemaker.

AM 10:14 Original letter, photographic copy, and typed transcript of letter, 15 February 1886, from Jefferson Davis, Beauvoir, MS, to the Senators and Representatives of Mississippi, regretting that he could not address them personally but urging them to establish some type of organized relief for needy Confederate veterans. Original ALS of 3 pages is mounted on boards. Donated by Lee Meriwether, St. Louis, MO, n.d.

AM 10:15 Xerox copy of typed transcript of will of Dr. Elisha Cullen Dick of Fairfax County, Virginia, dated 4 August 1813, and undated certificate of probate. Dr. Dick's role in attending President George Washington on his deathbed is explained by a xerox copy of an undated, twentieth century newspaper clipping.

AM 10:16. Carbon of a letter, 25 July 1926, from Juan Rayner of Pueblo, Colorado, to his sister concerning General Nathan Bedford Forrest's raid into Memphis during the Civil War.

AM 10:17. Handwritten court order, 4 December 1871, of the First Chancery Court of Shelby County, TN, concerning the consolidation of the Memphis and Charleston Railroad Company with the LaGrange and Memphis Railroad Company. Donated by Dr. and Mrs. W. S. Frances, 1 June 1969.

AM 10:18. Two folders of clippings and tearsheets on Memphis, TN, history from local newspapers, 1898-1964.

AM 10:19. Mimeographed list, undated, giving locations of General Nathan Bedford Forrest (CSA) and his troops in Tennessee, 1862-1865, indicating place, date, and division.

AM 10:20. Papers, 1965-1966, concerning a memorial service and unveiling of a highway marker in Crockett County, TN, for Thomas Conyers, Sr. (1757-1847), a Revolutionary War veteran who spent the latter part of his life in West Tennessee. The papers include directions to the marker, an invitation to the ceremony, a text of the marker, list of West Tennessee Historical Society members likely to attend, a program, and a clipping reporting on the event. There is also the text of the speech of Conyer's descendant, Dr. Sara Conyers Murray, at the dedication service, 15 August 1965, of the Lebanon Methodist Church in Crockett County, TN. In 1844 Conyers allowed the church to begin holding its services in his log cabin home. There is also a copy of Dr. Murray's history of the church, which she wrote in 1965. Donated by Dr. Sara Conyers Murray, Gates, TN, November 1965.

AM 10:21. Mimeographed genealogical information, "Descendants and Ancestors of Benjamin and Ann Frizelle Hooker," c. 1977. Donated by Malcolm D. Hooker, West Liberty, Ohio, 27 July 1977.

AM 10:22. Scrapbook of newspaper clippings, 1862, concerning the Civil War.

AM 10:23 Papers, 1901, n.d., concerning Judge John P. Young of Memphis; includes two obituaries, his poem, "The Mocking Bird's Song," and a ribbon from the eleventh reunion of the United Confederate Veterans, Memphis, 28-30 May 1901.

AM 10:24. Nineteen photographs of pages from *The Memphis Press-Scimitar* celebrating its sixtieth anniversary, 1940.

AM 10:25. Papers on the North Memphis Driving Park, once located in Memphis at Thomas and Maulden streets; includes original photographs, printed sketches of architectural features of the park, xerox copies and transparencies showing the park on city maps, and display material assembled by Charles Bobbitt (see his article on the park in the West Tennessee Historical Society *Papers*). Donated by Charles A. Bobbitt, Memphis, TN, 1977.

AM 10:26. Four copies of Tennessee landgrants, 1808-1827, concerning land in Middle and West Tennessee; includes positive and negative photostats, and a typed copy. Separated from the Marshall Wingfield Manuscripts (see AM 13).

AM 10:27. Papers, 1866, 1936, concerning the May, 1866, reconstruction riots in Memphis, TN; includes positive and negative photostats. Separated from the Marshall Wingfield Manuscripts (see AM 13).

AM 10:28. Two songs by Sabine Baring-Gould, "On the Resurrection Morning" and "Onward Christian, Soldiers". The collection is comprised of two photographs of manuscript copies prepared by two hands, n.d.

AM 10:29. Typed list of genealogical files held at the Goodwyn Institute, Memphis n.d.

AM 10:30. Typed copy of memorial to Mr. and Mrs. John Gaston of Memphis, read by Mr. J. J. Brenan at their tomb in Forrest Hill Cemetery, Memphis, December 1939.

AM 10:31. Playbill showing the Hopkins Stock Company playing at the New Lyceum Theatre, Memphis, TN, 1898-1899. Separated from the Marshall Wingfield Manuscripts (see AM 13).

AM 10:32. Miscellaneous papers concerning the Civil War; includes positive and negative photostats and xerox copies of an undated article on Confederate specie, two 1861 letters concerning the war, an 1864 resolution of re-enlistment of the members of the 154th Senior Regiment Tennessee Volunteers, and a typescript of the 1862-1864 diary of Lt. Perry Franklin Morgan of the 8th Tennessee Volunteer Infantry. Separated from the Marshall Wingfield Manuscripts (see AM 13).

AM 10:33. Negative photostat of a letter, 30 August 1875, from Nathan Bedford Forrest, Memphis, to Reuben Davis, Aberdeen, MS; concerns Forrest's search for a cannon requested by Davis.

AM 10:34. Papers, 1863-1954, concerning the Van Dorn-Peters Affair, 1863; includes a letter, 11 May 1863, to President Jefferson Davis concerning the shooting of General Earl Van Dorn (CSA) by Doctor George B. Peters for alleged improprieties with Mrs. Peters (the original is at the Duke Library). The papers also include a positive photostat, and transcripts containing additional information about this affair.

AM 10:35. Scrapbook, c. 1897-1920, of M. A. Marsh Family of Memphis; contains newspaper clippings of poems, photographs, general news items, and notices of births, deaths, and marriages.

AM 10:36. Scrapbook of clippings from Memphis newspapers, 1952-1955; contains local and world news of historical interst, and obituaries.

AM 10:37. Scrapbook of clippings from Memphis newspapers, 1933-1952; contains numerous columns by Memphian Paul Flowers, obituaries, and local and world news of historical interest.

AM 10:38. Scrapbook of clippings from Memphis newspapers, 1953-1955; includes obituaries of John D. Rust (the inventor of the mechanical cotton picker) [see AM 11] and others; and local news of historical interest.

AM 10:39. Scrapbook of clippings from Memphis newspapers, 1895, 1939-1952; includes photographs of city landmarks, society functions, and biographical articles or obituaries on important residents and visitors to Memphis like Jefferson and Varina Davis, Mark Twain, Eugene Magevney, John Gaston, Lee Meriwether, Bessie Vance

Brooks, Frederick Cossitt, Andrew Jackson, E. B. Ramsey, Billy Sunday, Gipsy Smith, Jr., Thomas Gailor, and others.

AM 10:40. Scrapbook of clippings from Memphis newspapers, 1951-1955; includes photographs of Southern mansions; biographical articles or obituaries on prominent Southerners like Elizabeth Avery Meriwether, William Orgill, Reuben Webster Millsaps, Amerigo Vespucci, Elizabeth Messick Houk, Ralph Davis, Thomas R. Watkins, an article on Randolph, TN, by Marshall Wingfield; and other local and world news of historical interest.

AM 10:41. Scrapbook of clippings from Memphis newspapers, 1900, 1921-1951; includes articles on the Ku Klux Klan by Mrs. George W. (Mary Hannah) Gordon (widow of the Klan's first Imperial Wizard); biographical articles about Virginia Frazer Boyle, George W. Gordon, and A. R. Porter; articles on the Civil War, the reunion of the N. B. Forrest Camp of the United Sons of Confederate Veterans in Memphis, and on the construction of Richard Halliburton's Chinese junk, the Sea Dragon.

AM 10:42. Scrapbook of clippings from Mid-South newspapers, 1929, 1938; includes articles on pilgrimages and exhibits of homes in Memphis, Natchez, and Holly Springs, Mississippi, the 1887 visit of President and Mrs. Grover Cleveland to Memphis, recollections of the yellow fever epidemics of the 1870's in Memphis, remembrances of the Civil War and its impact on Memphis' development, Memphis social functions, the naming of Beale Street in Memphis, Memphis' Overton Park Zoo, and obituaries of prominent Memphians.

AM 10:43. Scrapbook containing manuscript of a poem, 1877, and clippings from Memphis newspapers, 1938-1951; includes articles on Memphis social functions; biographical articles and obituaries on prominent Memphians like Mrs. A. B. Pickett, Marie Greenwood Worden, Irvin S. Cobb, and Thomas Gailor; articles on meetings of Confederate veterans, pilgrimages and exhibits of historic homes in Memphis and La Grange, TN, and in Natchez and Greenville, MS, on the impact of Memphis' private schools, and on the award of the Nobel Prize for Literature to novelist William Faulkner. There is also a negative photostat copy of a Patrick Henry landgrant, 18 May 1786, the original of which is catalogued as AM 10:49.

AM 10:44. Scrapbook of clippings from Memphis newspapers, 1933-1952; includes articles on the changing currents of the lower Mississippi River, the history of Memphis postal service, Memphis social functions including the annual Cotton Carnival, Memphis street cars, recollections of the Civil War, the banishment of Elizabeth

Avery Meriwether from Memphis, the birth of her child Lee, reunions of Confederate veterans, the ceremonies at which William Faulkner was awarded the Nobel Prize for Literature, an account by a Memphis woman of her life in Nazi-occupied Norway during World War II, a history of Tupelo, Mississippi, the Lyceum Theatre in Memphis, actress Lillian Russell, and Memphis cemeteries and significant buildings. There are also biographical articles and obituaries on such noted Southerners or visitors as Frederick Cossitt, Thomas Gailor, Anne Sullivan Macy, and Sam Jones.

AM 10:45. Scrapbook of clippings from Memphis newspapers, 1942-1954; includes articles on Memphis postal service, Memphis social functions including the 50th wedding anniversary of Mr. and Mrs. E. H. Crump, the poems of Virginia Frazer Boyle, historic homes in Memphis and elsewhere in the mid-south, Lee Meriwether's observations on the historic changes in penal methods in Lisbon, Portugal, the likeness of Memphis' E. H. Crump on *Time* magazine's cover, the poetry of Memphian Walter Malone, Memphis cemeteries, the history of Memphis real estate (featuring the accomplishments of George W. Person, Rowlett Paine, and E. O. Bailey), settling the estate of Texas multi-millionaire William Lewis Moddy, Jr., tributes to Memphian Dr. Marshall Wingfield the succession to the throne of England by Queen Elizabeth II, the Tom Lee Memorial in Memphis, and biographical articles or obituaries on Marie Greenwood Worden, Dorothy Dix, Jefferson Davis, and James Zachariah George.

AM 10:46. Scrapbook of clippings from Memphis newspapers, 1938-1942, with clippings arranged by year in overlapping layers on each page. Topics include the athletics program and the students at Memphis schools—especially at the West Tennessee State Teachers College (later Memphis State College). There is also information on Memphis social and entertainment functions, and Memphians serving the war effort in the armed services and on the home front.

AM 10:47. Handwritten summary of the 23 June 1823, decision by the Tennessee Supreme Court of Errors and Appeals, meeting in Charlotte, TN in the case of James Mallory of Stewart County, TN vs. John Smith. Donated by Mrs. Bertie Shaw Rollins, n.p., n.d.

AM 10:48. Printed $1000 bond of the State of Tennessee signed 1 June 1861 by Governor Isham Harris with nineteen interest coupons signed by Controller F. T. Dunlap; a faint impression of the state seal still remains. Interest on the bond was 8% annually, payable semiannually.

AM 10:49. Land grant, 18 May 1786, signed by Patrick Henry, Governor of Virginia, transferring 500 acres of land in Fayette County to Geddes Winston. See negative photostatic copy mounted in scrapbook (AM 10:43). Donated by Lee Meriwether, St. Louis, MO, n.d. n.d.

AM 10:50. Letter, 18 April 1867, from Robert E. Lee, Lexington, VA to Heber W. Jones, Somerville, TN counselling him concerning his preparation for admittance to school. The letter is framed in wood under glass with its stamped envelope, also in Lee's hand.

AM 11. *Rust, John D. Papers*, 1933-1953. 1 container, totalling .3 cu. ft. Papers, 1933-1953, of a Memphis inventor of a mechanical cotton picker, including his 1952 paper on "The Origin and Development of the Cotton Picker", outlining the history of mechanization in cotton farming and his own attempts to develop and market an efficient, inexpensive cotton picking machine. There are also printed drawings of machines Rust patented between 1933 and 1953. Additional information on the Rust Family is available in the Marshall Wingfield Papers (AM 13). Provenance unknown.

AM 12. *Saint, John C.* (1820-1903) *Papers*, 1846—1870. 1 container totalling .3 cu. ft.
Papers of a wealthy Memphis entrepreneur, 1846-1870; includes correspondence, invitations, genealogical information on the Saint Family, deeds, state and Shelby County tax records, blueprints of his property in Shelby County, receipts, grocery orders, clippings, and a c. 1870 three dimensional drawing of a patented Harrison washing machine, for which Saint won a prize in 1869. The correspondence contains both business and personal letters concerning his cotton and real estate businesses, his slaveholding, and ordinary family and social matters. These papers reveal that following the Civil War, he returned to Memphis to rebuild successfully his fortune. In the early 1950s this collection was donated as part of the Woodson Family Collection (see AM 14) by Dr. Alice Woodson Cameron, a granddaughter of John C. Saint, of Memphis, TN, but was separated sometime after that date.

AM 13. *Wingfield, Marshall* (1893-1961). *Papers*, 1939-1963. 1 container, totalling 1 cu. ft.
Papers, 1939-1963, of a minister, author, historian, and president of the Historical Society. Arranged in four series, the collection includes a correspondence file, a subject file, works written by Dr. Wingfield, and clippings and pamphlets he collected. The general correspondence relates to his work as a minister of the Christian Church at Memphis' First Congregational Church, his civic activities in Memphis, and his historical research. It also documents his longtime friendship with John D. Rust (see AM 11) and with Lee Meriwether

(see AM 9). The subject files reveal details of his work with the Memphis Christian Mission, the Council of Churches in Memphis and at state, national, and world levels, the Civil War Centennial in Tennessee, clippings and photographs concerning Sam Houston, his Bible, and other artifacts connected with him and his family, and Dr. Wingfield's other activities. In another series are an extensive bibliography of Dr. Wingfield's reviews and writings as well as copies of some speeches and writings on religious and historical topics. Two folders contain pamphlets and unsorted clippings he saved. Numerous photographs, pamphlets, books, artifacts, and miscellaneous manuscripts were separated from these papers to other sections of the West Tennessee Historical Society collection. Provenance unknown. Five cubic feet of files donated on 31 Aug 1978, by Mrs. Marshall Wingfield, are still unprocessed.

AM 14. *Woodson Family. Papers*, c. 1800, 1857-1916. 1 container, totalling .3 cu. ft.

Personal and business papers of a Shelby County father and son, John Morton Woodson (1821-after 1871) and Henry Morton Woodson (1845-?), including genealogical information on the Woodson and Saint Families; routine business papers of John Morton Woodson, 1856-1965; and business and personal papers of Henry Morton Woodson who manufactured cotton gins in Germantown, TN until the factory was burned early in the Civil War. The papers include an 1865 furlough that Confederate soldier H. M. Woodson received after swearing "not to take up any military duty whatsoever", and a large number of personal letters (carbon copies) he wrote concerning matters of local interest, including the yellow fever epidemics of the late 1870's, the distaste Southern women had for travelling unaccompanied, and a 1914 review of a book on carpetbaggers. The collection also contains a manuscript entitled "Unlawful Marriages", c. 1800, with a "table of kindred and affinity" indicating relationships within a family that will allow marriage. Donated by Dr. Alice Woodson Cameron, daughter of H. W. Woodson, in the early 1950s; following the donation, the John C. Saint Papers (see AM 12) were separated from this collection.

2
BOOKS

B1 Thomas Benjamin Alexander. *Thomas A. R. Nelson of East Tennessee.* Nashville: Tennessee Historical Commission, 1956.

B2 American Historical Association. *Annual Report,* volume 1 (1935) and v. 2 (1899). Washington, D.C.: U. S. Government Printing Office, 1890-

B3 William James Bacon. *History of the Fifty-fifth Field Artillery Brigade.* Nashville, TN: Benson Printing Company, 1920.

B4 Thomas Harrison Baker. *The Memphis Commercial Appeal.* Baton Rouge, LA: Louisiana State University Press, 1971.

B5 Mrs. Kate Trader Barrow. *A Happy House of Life, and Other Verses.* Memphis, TN: S. C. Toof and Company, 1941.

B6 Ben M. Barrus, Milton L. Baughn, and Thomas H. Campbell. *A People Called Cumberland Presbyterians.* Memphis, TN: Frontier Press, 1972.

B7 Ella C. Bennett. *Abelard & Heloise.* San Francisco and New York: P. Elder & Company, 1907.

B8 *The Bible.* Edinburgh: Alexander Kincaid, 1769.

B9 Jean Patterson Bible. *Melungeons Yesterday and Today.* Jefferson City, TN: Bible, c. 1975.

B10 William Blount. *The Blount Journal, 1790—1796.* Nashville, TN: Benson Printing Company, 1955.

B11 Virginia Frazer Boyle. *The Other Side.* Cambridge: Riverside Press, 1893.

B12 Carl W. Breihan. *Quantrill and His Civil War Guerrillas.* Denver: Sage Books, 1959.

B13 Geraldine Brooks. *Dames and Daughters of Colonial Days.* New York, NY: T. Y. Crowell & Company, 1900.

B14 Virginia Feild Walton Brooks. *Screed of Safari Scribe.* Memphis, TN: c. 1947.

B15 Gerald Mortimer Capers. *The Mississippi River: Before and After Mark Twain.* Hicksville, NY: Exposition Press, 1977.

B16 Gerald Mortimer Capers. *The Biography of a River Town; Memphis: Its Heroic Age.* New Orleans, LA: 1966.

B17 Robert Catlett Cave. *The Men in Gray.* Nashville, TN: Confederate Veteran, 1911.

B18 Gifford Alexander Cochran. *Grandeur in Tennessee.* New York: J. J. Augustin, 1946.

B19 *The Commercial Appeal. Centennial Edition 1840—1940.* Memphis, TN: 1940.

B20 Clara Conway. *Silver—lined Days*. Memphis, TN: Paul & Douglas, 1902.

B21 Waller Raymond Cooper. *Southwestern at Memphis, 1848—1948*. Richmond: John Knox Press, 1949.

B22 Jabez Lamar Monroe Curry. *Civil History of the Government of the Confederate States*. Richmond, VA: B. F. Johnson Publishing Company, 1901.

B23 Ellen Davies-Rodgers. *The Great Book: Calvary Protestant Episcopal Church, 1832—1972*. Memphis, TN: Plantation Press, 1973.

B24 Ellen Davies-Rodgers. *The Holy Innocents*. Brunswick, TN: Plantation Press, 1965.

B25 James D. Davis. *History of Memphis*. Memphis, TN: West Tennessee Historical Society, 1972.

B26 John Henry Davis. *St. Mary's Cathedral, 1858—1958*. Memphis, TN: Chapter of St. Mary's Cathedral, 1958.

B27 Varina Howell Davis. *Jefferson Davis*. New York: Belford Company, 1890.

B28 Eva Tucker Denton. *Each Day A Bonus*. Tunica, MS: Mississippi Plantation Press, 1966.

B29 Kenneth Graham Duffield. *Bill of the U.S.A*. Philadelphia: Henry Altemus Company, 1918.

B30 Dwight Lowell Dumond. *America in Our Time, 1896—1946*. New York: H. Holt and Company, 1947.

B31 Ruth Henley Duncan. *The Captain and Submarine CSS H. L. Hunley*. Memphis (?): 1965.

B32 Mabel Flannigan Edrington. *History of Mississippi County, Arkansas*. Ocala, FL: 1962.

B33 George Cary Eggleston. *The History of the Confederate War*. New York: Sturgis and Walton Company, 1910.

B34 Clement Anselm Evans. *Confederate Military History*. Atlanta, GA: Confederate Publishing Company, 1899.

B35 James Rutherford Fair. *The North Arkansas Line*. Berkeley, CA: Howwell—North Books, 1969.

B36 Charles H. Faulkner. *The Old Stone Fort*. Knoxville, TN: University of Tennessee Press, 1968.

B37 Federal Writers' Project. *Tennessee*. New York: The Viking Press, 1939.

B38 Stanley John Folmsbee, Robert E. Corlew, and Enoch L. Mitchell. *Tennessee*. Knoxville, TN: University of Tennessee Press, 1969.

B39 Jesse Hill Ford. *The Liberation of Lord Byron Jones*. Boston: Little, Brown, 1965.

B40 Rebel C. Forrester. *Glory and Tears*. Union City, TN: H. A. Lanzer Company, 1970.

B41 George Towns Gaines. *Fighting Tennesseans*. Kingsport, TN: Kingsport Press, 1931.

B42 *Goodspeed's History of Hamilton, Knox and Shelby Counties of Ten-*

nessee. Nashville, TN: Charles and Randy Elder, Booksellers, 1974. Reprinted from Goodspeed's History, 1887.

B43 Lee Seifert Greene and Robert Sterling Avery. *Government in Tennessee.* Knoxville, TN: University of Tennessee Press, 1962.

B44 William Brown Griffing. *Poems by William Brown Griffing.* Tokyo: 1912.

B45 John Brice Harris. *From Old Mobile to Fort Assumption.* Nashville, TN: Parthenon Press, 1959.

B46 John Haywood. *The Civil and Political History of the State of Tennessee From Its Earliest Settlement Up To The Year 1796.* Knoxville, TN: Tenase Company, 1969.

B47 Burton Jesse Hendrick. *Statesmen of the Lost Cause.* New York: Literary Guild of America, 1939.

B48 Robert Selph Henry. *As They Saw Forrest.* Jackson, TN: McCowat-Mercer Press, 1956.

B49 Stanley Fitzgerald Horn. *Invisible Empire.* Boston, MA: Houghton Mifflin Company, 1939.

B50 Stanley Fitzgerald Horn. *Invisible Empire.* Cos Cob, CT: J. E. Edwards, 1969.

B51 John Milton Hubbard. *Notes of a Private.* Memphis, TN: E. H. Clarke and Brother, 1909.

B52 Clifton E. Hull. *Shortline Railroads of Arkansas.* Norman, OK: University of Oklahoma Press, 1969.

B53 Thomas Jefferson. *The Writings of Thomas Jefferson.* Washington, D.C.: Thomas Jefferson Memorial Association of the U.S., 1905.

B54 Thomas Jordan. *The Campaigns of Lieut. Gen. N. B. Forrest.* Dayton, Ohio: Morningside Bookshop, 1973.

B55 John McLeod Keating. *History of the City of Memphis and Shelby County, Tennessee.* Syracuse, NY: D. Mason and Company, 1888. Reprinted by Burke's Book Store and Frank and Gennie Myers, Memphis, TN, 1977.

B56 Benjamin La Bree. *The Confederate Soldier in the Civil War.* Paterson, NJ: Pageant Books, 1959.

B57 Melvin Gunnard Larson. *Mud 'n' Mercy in Memphis.* Wheaton, IL: Van Kampen Press, 1955.

B58 Melvin Gunnard Larson. *Skid Row Stopgap.* Wheaton, IL: Van Kampen Press, 1950.

B59 The Lavonia Times. *History of Franklin County, Georgia.* Lavonia, GA: 1934.

B60 George Washington Lee. *Beale Street.* College Park, MD: McGrath Publishing Company, 1969.

B61 George Washington Lee. *Beale Street Sundown.* New York: House of Field, c 1942.

B62 George Washington Lee. *River George.* New York: The Macaulay Company, 1937.

B63 Mrs. Mary Ashton Livermore. *My Story of the War*. Hartford: A. D. Worthington and Company, 1888.
B64 N. M. Long. *Sermons and Addresses*. Memphis, TN: S. C. Toof and Company, 1906.
B65 William David McCain. *Memoirs of Henry Tillinghast Ireys*. Jackson, MS: Mississippi Department of Archives and History, 1954.
B66 Iris Hopkins McClain. *A History of Houston County*. Columbia, TN: 1966.
B67 Anna Leigh McCorkle. *Tales of Old Whitehaven*. Jackson, TN: McCowat-Mercer Press, 1967.
B68 William Holmes McGuffey. *McGuffey's Eclectic Reader*. Rev. ed. New York, Cincinnati: American Book Company, 1879.
B69 Shields McIlwaine. *Memphis Down in Dixie*. New York: E. P. Dutton, 1948.
B70 *Memphis. Elmwood Cemetery*. Memphis, TN: Boyle and Chapman, 1874.
B71 Elizabeth Avery Meriwether. *The Master of Red Leaf*. New York: E. J. Hale and Son, 1880.
B72 Elizabeth Avery Meriwether. *Recollections of 92 Years, 1824—1916*. Nashville, TN: Tennessee Historical Commission, 1958.
B73 Lee Meriwether. *After Thoughts, a Sequel to My Yesteryears*. Webster Groves, MO: International Mark Twain Society, 1945.
B74 Lee Meriwether. *Europe Now and Then*. Webster Groves, MO: International Mark Twain Society, 1951.
B75 Lee Meriwether. *More Yesteryears*. Columbia, MO: Artcraft Press, 1955.
B76 Lee Meriwether. *My First 98 Years, 1962—1960*. Columbia, MO: Artcraft Press, 1960.
B77 Lee Meriwether. *My First 100 Years*. St. Louis, MO: 1963.
B78 Lee Meriwether. *My Yesteryears*. Webster Groves, MO: The International Mark Twain Society, 1942.
B79 Lee Meriwether. *The War Diary of a Diplomat*. New York: Dodd, Mead and Company, 1919.
B80 Minor Meriwether.*Lineage of the Meriwethers and the Minors From Colonial Times*. St. Louis: Nixon—Jones Print Co., 1895.
B81 William D. Miller. *Memphis During the Progressive Era, 1900—1917*. Memphis, TN: Memphis State University Press, 1957.
B82 William D. Miller. *Mr. Crump of Memphis*. Baton Rouge, LA: Louisiana State University Press, 1964.
B83 John Trotwood Moore. *Tennessee, The Volunteer State, 1769—1923.*. Chicago, Nashville: The S. J. Clarke Publishing Company, 1923.
B84 Dorotha O. Norton. *Kenton: Folklore and Fact* Kenton, TN: Kenton Jaycettes, 1972.
B85 John Robertson Pepper. *Well—nigh 50 Years at the Superintendent's Desk*. Memphis, TN: Press of Early-Freeburg Company, 1929.
B86 Kate Johnston Peters. *Lauderdale County From Earliest Times*. Ripley, TN: Sugar Hill Lauderdale County Library, 1957.

B87 Ulrich Bonnell Phillips. *Life and Labor in the Old South*. Boston: Little, Brown, 1951.
B88 Clark Porteous. *The First Orgill Century, 1847—1947*. Memphis, TN: M. Kremer, Inc., 1947.
B89 Edward Payson Powell. *Nullification and Secession in the United States*. New York: G. P. Putnam's Sons, 1898.
B90 James Gettys McGready Ramsey. *The Annals of Tennessee to the End of the Eighteenth Century*. Knoxville, TN: East Tennessee Historical Society, 1967.
B91 Eldon Roark. *Memphis Bragabouts*. New York, London: Whittlesey House, McGraw-Hill Book Company, Inc., 1945.
B92 Ellen Davies Rodgers. *The Romance of the Episcopal Church in West Tennessee*. Brunswick, TN: Plantation Press, 1964.
B93 James Roper. *The Founding of Memphis, 1818—1820*. Memphis, TN: Memphis Sesquicentennial, Inc., 1970.
B94 Mary Utopia Rothrock. *Discovering Tennessee*. Knoxville, TN: Mary U. Rothrock, 1955.
B95 Silas Erwin Scates. *A School History of Tennessee*. Yonkers-on-Hudson, NY, Chicago: World Book Company, 1925.
B96 Samuel Shankman. *Baron Hirsch Congregation*. Memphis, TN: 1957.
B97 *Sign—On: The First 50 Years of WREC Radio*. Memphis, TN: 1972.
B98 William Gilmore Simms. *War Poetry of the South*. New York: Richardson and Company, 1867.
B99 Algie Martin Simons. *Social Forces in American History*. New York: The Macmillan Company, 1911.
B100 William Wright Sorrels. *Memphis' Greatest Debate*. Memphis, TN: Memphis State University Press, 1970.
B101 *The South in the Building of the Nation*. Richmond, VA: The Southern Historical Publication Society, 1909—1913.
B102 Southern Historical Society. *Southern Historical Society Papers*. vol. 8 (1880) and 14 (1886). Richmond, VA.
B103 *The Southerner*. New Orleans, LA: Southern Editors Association, 1944.
B104 Alexander Hamilton Stephens. *A Constitutional View of the Late War Between the States*. Philadelphia, PA: National Publishing Company, Chicago, IL: Zeigler, McCurdy and Company, 1868-70.
B105 Hudson Strode. *Jefferson Davis*. New York: Harcourt, Brace, 1955.
B106 Charles Albert Stuck. *The Story of Craighead County*. Jonesboro, AR: 1960.
B107 John Leisk Tait. *Art Work of Memphis*. Chicago: Gravure Illustration Company, 1912.
B108 Robert Talley. *One Hundred Years of the Commercial Appeal*. Memphis, TN: Commerical Appeal, 1940.
B109 Robert H. White. *Messages of the Governors of Tennessee*. Nashville, TN: Tennessee Historical Commission, 1952.
B110 *Tennessee, Commission Book, 1796—1801*. Nashville, TN: Tennessee Historical Commission, 1957.

B111 *Tennessee State Federation of Women's Clubs.* Memphis, TN: Jones—Briggs Company, 1916.

B112 A. Tracy. *Dear Little Marchioness.* Boston: C. J. Peters and Son, c. 1894.

B113 *Trinity United Methodist Church, Memphis.* Memphis, TN: History Writing Committee, 1975.

B114 David M. Tucker. *Lieutenant Lee of Beale Street.* Nashville, TN: Vanderbilt University Press, 1971.

B115 *U.S. Bureau of American Ethnology.* Washington, DC: Government Printing Office, 1881—1915.

B116 U.S. Fifty—First Congress, second session. *Memorial Addresses on the Life and Character of James Phelan.* Washington, DC: Government Printing Office, 1891.

B117 U.S. Naval War Records Office. *Offical Records of the Union and Confederate Navies in the War of the Rebellion.* Washington, DC: Government Printing Office, 1894—1927.

B118 United States 70th Congress, first session. *Acceptance and Unveiling of the Statue of Andrew Jackson.* Washington, DC: Government Printin Office. 1929.

B119 U.S. War Department. *The War of the Rebellion* . Washington, DC: Government Printing Office, 1880—1901.

B120 Paul J. Vanderwood. *Night Riders of Reelfoot Lake.* Memphis, TN: Memphis State University Press, 1969.

B121 John Vaught. *Rebel Coach.* Memphis, TN: Memphis State University Press, 1971.

B122 Thomas Isaac Wharton. *A Digested Index to the Reported Decisions of the Several Courts of Law in the United States.* Philadelphia: H. C. Carey and I. Lea, 1824.

B123 Emma Inman Williams. *Historic Madison.* Jackson, TN: Madison County Historical Society, 1946.

B124 Samuel Cole Williams. *Beginnings of West Tennessee.* Nashville, TN: Blue and Gray Press, 1971.

B125 Marshall Wingfield. *Literary Memphis.* Memphis, TN: The West Tennessee Historical Society, 1942.

B126 Marshall Wingfield. *An Old Virginia Court.* Memphis, TN: West Tennessee Historical Society, 1948.

B127 Marshall Wingfield. *The Shrine in a Temple* Memphis, TN: Al Chymia Temple, A.A.O.N.M.S., 1943.

B128 John Preston Young. *Standard History of Memphis, Tennessee.* Evansville, IN: Unigraphic, Inc. 1974. Reprint of the 1912 edition by the West Tennessee Historical Society.

B129 Waldo Zimmermann. *The Dog Who Came To Dinner.* Memphis, TN: Rusty Guardsman Memorial Foundation, 1956.

PHOTOGRAPHS AND IMAGES

DAGUERROTYPES:

Ph 1. Handcolored daguerrotype of parents of General G. W. Gordon, n.d., mounted in embossed leather case, 9 x 12 cm. Presented by Alma Ramsey Bowers, Memphis, 1 Jan 1957.

TINTYPES:

Ph 2. Tintype of unidentified young soldier, c. 1861, mounted in embossed leather case with broken hinge, 8 x 9 cm. Inscribed faintly on back of copper frame is "My sweetheart/He is as nice as a/Pie—Yes, he is that/ (illegible)." Separated from Marshall Wingfield Manuscripts (see AM 13).

Ph 3. Tintype of group of men, a woman, and a child standing on porch of unidentified store, n.d., not in case, 9 x 12 cm.

Ph 4. Handcolored tintype of two little girls, one identified as "My mother at about 7 yrs. Memphis. Ella Costillo," c. 1872, mounted in embossed leather case with broken hinge, 9 x 8 cm. Separated from Ella Costillo Bennett Manuscripts (see AM 3).

Ph 5. Handcolored tintype of a young woman, n.d., mounted in embossed leather case, 7 x 6 cm. Labelled "We think Amelia—grandmother Doyle's sister who married a steamboat clerk and went to St. Louis to live and died within a year. (My Aunt's memoirs) p. 7." Separated from Ella Costillo Bennett Manuscripts (see AM 3).

PHOTOGRAPHS:

Ph 6. Paperprint of Michael Charles Costillo, n.d., mounted in embossed leather case, 12 x 9½ cm. Ribbon imprinted "Central Committee" is also in the case. Labelled as "Grandfather Michael Chas. Costillo: Born Tipperary, Ire. Died in Memphis of yellow fever. Epidemic of 1878. Vice chairman of the Democratic Committee during the Civil War and noted horseman. Antislavery advocate and friend of Parson Brownlow, Edotor (sic) of the Knoxville Whig." Further identified as "copied from a painting done by Prof. Clarke who was in the South painting family portraits before the war—but was called back to Europe before he was able to paint a portrait of my mother. See memoirs, p. 33, 50, 65." Separated from the Ella Costillo Bennett Manuscripts (see AM 3).

Ph 7. Handcolored paperprint of Ellen Doyle Costillo, n.d., in pressed gutta perche case, 9 x 8 cm. Labelled as "Ellen Doyle Costillo—wife of Michael Chas. Costillo—Born Co Tipperary, Ire. married Memphis—1858—Died in (illegible) around 1881 (memoirs, p. 5)." Separated from Ella Costillo Bennett Manuscripts (see AM 3).

Ph 8. Paperprint of George Sexton Bennett, n.d., in pressed gutta perche case, 9 x 8 cm. Labelled as "My father Geo. Sexton Bennett born near Lexington, Kentucky. Possibly fraudulent (he didn't know). Parents died very young—father was Editor of *Cincinnati Inquirer* and for brief period *Louisville Courier* (memoirs—p. 101)." Separated from Ella Costillo Bennett Manuscripts (see AM 3).

Ph 9. Paperprint of Ella Costillo Bennett, Denver, Colorado, 1883, mounted in embossed leather case, 9 x 8 cm. Labelled on back of print as "Ella Costillo Bennett. Born Memphis Tennessee, 1865. Died L. A. California, 1932." Separate label further states her age as 18 at time of photograph in Denver and refers to memoirs, p. 98. Separated from Ella Costillo Bennett Manuscripts (see AM 3).

Ph 10. Paperprint of Mary (Mollie) Costillo Bennett with her first child Winnie Lou, c. 1880, mounted in pressed gutta perche case, 9 x 8 cm. Mary Bennett was born in Memphis, TN in 1859 and died in Walsenburg, Colorado, c. 1947. Duplicated by Ph 22, this was separated from Ella Costillo Bennett Manuscripts (see AM 3).

Ph 11. Paperprint of Raphael Fabian Bennett as a child, c. 1890, mounted in embossed leather case, 9 x 8 cm. Labelled in case behind print as "Raphael Fabian Bennett. Born Portland Oregon, 1895. Son of Ella Costillo Bennett. [Ella was a] former feature writer on *Portland Oregonian, Denver Post* and St. Louis Papers—poet, dramatic critic and editorial writer—author of "Love Letters of Abelard and Heloise" —Publisher Paul Elder and Company, San Francisco (California) 1907." Separate label further states that he was "Ella's youngest son named after Adm. Raphael Semmes." Separated from Ella Costillo Bennett Manuscripts (see AM 3).

Ph 12. Paperprint of Mary L. Bennett of Los Angeles, c. 1890, mounted in embossed leather case, 9 x 8 cm. Separated from Ella Costillo Bennett Manuscripts (see AM 3).

Ph 13. Handcolored paperprint of "Capt. Raphael Semmes, C.S.A.," n.d., mounted in pressed gutta perche case, 7½ x 6 cm. Separated from Ella Costillo Bennett Manuscripts (see AM 3).

Ph 14. Photographic portrait of Ella Costillo Bennett, San Francisco, 1905. Photographer: Arnold Geuthe. Framed in wood under glass, 25 x 19 cm. Identification written on back of frame and attached to glass. Separated from Ella Costillo Bennett Manuscripts (see AM 3).

Ph 15. Photograph of Jefferson Davis, 1880's, mounted on board, 16½ x 10½ cm. Photographer: J. H. Moyston, 338 Main Street, Memphis, TN. Donated by Alma Ramsey Bowers, Memphis, 1 Jan 1957.

Ph 16. Faded photograph of Jefferson Davis, c. 1883, mounted on board, repaired in lower right corner with scotch tape, 16½ cm. x 10½ cm. Photographer: G. Moses, 121 Canal Street, New Orleans, La. Provenance unknown.

Ph 17. Portrait of Bishop Thomas Gailor of Memphis clipped from magazine, n.d., glued on back of mounted photograph of unidentified young woman, c. 1900. Board, 35 x 25½ cm. The Gailor portrait is brittle; the photo of the woman is faded; and the board has been punctured in upper corner and bears stains of glue and scotch tape. Donated by Alma Ramsey Bowers, Memphis, 1 Jan 1957.

Ph 18. Faded photograph of George W. Gordon, late in his life, mounted on board, 20 x 15 cm. Photographer: Gray of Memphis. Labelled "Geo. W. Gordon, Brigadier General C.S.A. 1864." Donated by Alma Ramsey Bowers Memphis, 1 Jan 1957.

Ph 19. Faded photograph of Mamie H. Gordon, n.d., mounted on board, 39½ x 24 cm. This portrait of Mrs. George W. Gordon may date from her school days; beneath the photo is a handwritten list of some of her teachers and schoolmates. Provenance unknown.

Ph 20. Faded photograph of G. W. Jones of Middle Tennessee, n.d., mounted on board, 10 x 6½ cm. Photographer: Carl C. Giers, Nashville, TN, negative number 31737. Donated with a letter of genealogical information by Mrs. W. B. Cowan, Memphis, 7 January 1958.

Ph 21. Positive photostatic copy of photograph of Robert E. Lee and his signature "R. E. Lee", c. 1865, framed under glass, 58 x 41 cm. Donated by Alma Ramsey Bowers, Memphis 1 Jan 1957.

Ph 22. Photograph of Mary Costillo and Winnie Lou Nichols, Denver, c. 1880, 15½ x 11 cm. Labelled on back "Mollie Costillo Nickolds (sic). Left Memphis, 1879—Married in St. Louis—Left for Chicago and then out to Denver and in 1880—where her 1st child—Winnie Lou was born—Taken in Denver with Winnie—who is now in her late 70's and in a rest home in Fresno." Duplicate of Ph 10. Separated from the Ella Costillo Bennett Manuscripts (see AM 3).

Ph 23. Photograph of John C. Saint late in his life, n.d., mounted on board, 18½ x 13½ cm. Separated from John C. Saint Manuscripts (see AM 12).

Ph 24. Torn, faded photograph of Mary Jane Smyth, n.d., mounted on damaged board roughly 21 x 20 cm. Provenance unknown.

Ph 25. Three photographs of United Confederate Veterans' reunions:
1.) Colonel Richard P. Lake leading march down Main Street, Memphis, c. 1909; not mounted, 16½ x 11½ cm.

2.) Statue of General Stephen D. Lee at Vicksburg, from 1911 reunion; mounted on board, 20 x 15 cm.
3.) Richard P. Lake riding down Pontotoc Street, Memphis, 1913. Inscribed "Compliments of Richard P. Lake, Asst. Adjt. Gen. UCV. Mounted on 'Whitney', descendent of Forrest's Cavalry and Union's Federal Cavalry strain. May 1913". Provenance unknown.

Ph 26. Faded photograph of Corporal Wilder (USA), c. 1862, mounted on board 16½ x 11 cm. Inscribed on back, "Corporal Wilder, the Federal Soldier who captured me near Tazewell, Tenn in 1862. Geo. W. Gordon" in Gordon's hand. Donated by Alma Ramsey Bowers, Memphis, 1 Jan 1957.

Ph 27. Three photographs of Marshall Wingfield:
1.) Dr. Wingfield in a group photo at the unveiling of monument to David Crockett, Trenton, TN, 13 Oct 1950. Also included are Gov. Browning, Seale Johnson, Dr. Robison, Judge Bejach, Mrs. J. H. DeWitt, Mrs. Belle Kenney Scholz (the sculptor of the bronze bust of Crockett), Col. Charles Tipps of Dallas, TX, Col. Temple Houston Morrow (grandson of Sam Houston) and J. D. Pate (great—great grandson of Crockett). Not mounted; 24 x 19 cm. 2.) Dr. Wingfield presiding over military exercises at Shiloh battlefield on 90th anniversary of the battle, 6 April 1952. Not mounted, 12½ x 9 cm.
3.) Portrait of Dr. Wingfield in his later years, n.d. Separated from the Marshall Wingfield Manuscripts (see AM 13).

Ph 28. Photograph of unidentified man, mid—19th century, mounted on board, 10 x 6 cm. Provenance unknown.

Ph 29. Seven photographs of speakers and audience at Shiloh National Military Park on 90th anniversary of the battle, 6 April 1952. 3 black and white prints, loose, 12½ x 9 cm. 4 faded color prints, loose, 14½ x 9 cm. Separated from Marshall Wingfield Manuscripts (see AM 13).

Ph 30. Three faded color photographs of Tennessee Historical Commission highway markers in place on the road, 1952, loose, 14½ x 9 cm. Markers include "McNairy County", "Old Stagecoach Inn", and "Purdy". Possibly separated from Marshall Wingfield Manuscripts (see AM 13).

Ph 31. Color postcard of Dr. B. V. Hudson Home, Bolivar, TN, c. 1950. 14 x 9 cm. Provenance unknown.

Ph 32. Black and white postcard of "The Briers", Natchez, MS, early 20th century. 14 x 9 cm. Mrs. Jefferson Davis was raised and married in this house. Provenance unknown.

ENGRAVINGS:
Ph 33. Five black and white portraits of Civil War figures, n.d., 9 x 6 cm., by C. Prang and Co., Boston, Massachusetts. Includes "John Slidell",

"General Price", "General Sherman", "General Thomas" and "Lieut. General U. S. Grant". Possibly donated to West Tennessee Historical Society by Mrs. W. B. Cowan, Memphis, 7 Jan 1958.

Ph 34. Colored engraving, "Death of General Andrew Jackson", copyright 1845 by N. Currier. Torn and mounted on brown paper and cardboard, 36 x 25½ cm. Donated by Mrs. Doyle Stubblefield, Houston, MS, 12 February 1958.

Ph 35. Black and white certificate of donation to the Southern monument at Richmond, Virginia in honor of Jefferson Davis and all his associates in the Confederacy, n.d., framed under glass, 74 x 57 cm. Copyrighted and published by Clarke-Art Engraving Company, Philadelphia, PA and Atlanta, GA; copied from the original by Levytype Company, Philadelphia, PA. Provenance unknown.

LITHOGRAPHS:
Ph 36. Brittle, color lithograph of four flags of Confederacy and Confederate organizations, n.d. Loose, 27½ x 22½ cm. Printed identification on back reads "Sold for benefit of Davis monument. Mrs. W. M. Robert Vawter, compiler, Richmond chapter." Provenance unknown.

WATERCOLORS:
Ph 37. Watercolor of three flags of the Confederacy, n.d., framed in wood under glass, 27 x 21½ cm. Pencilled on back of frame is almost illegible explanation of the different uses of the flags. Donated by Alma Ramsey Bowers, Memphis, 1 Jan 1957.

OIL PAINTING:
Ph 38. Oil painting on cloth of a man, possibly Thomas Bradford Carroll, Mayor of Memphis from July 1856 until his death on 28 April 1857, framed in wood, 119 x 101 cm. Provenance unknown.

4
PERIODICALS

Provenance generally unknown, but those titles marked by asterisk donated with the Ella Costillo Bennett manuscripts (See AM 3).

P. 1. *The American Woman*, vol. 15, no. 3 (Aug 1905). Augusta, Maine: Vickery & Hill Publishing Company. 40 cm. monthly. Condition—fragile.

P. 2. *Bulletin of the Institute of Historical Research*, 55th Annual Report (1 Aug 1975-31 July 1976); vol. 49, no. 120 (Nov 1976) and special supplement no. 11; vol. 50, no. 121 and 122 (May-Nov 1977). London, England: Institute of Historical Research University of London. 25 cm. semi—annually. Condition—excellent.

P. 3. *Collier's*, vol. 26, no. 18, 22, 24, 25; vol. 27, no. 2, 5, 11, 12, 16, 17, 22, 24, 26; vol. 28, no. 6, 11, 12, 14, 15, 17 (2 Feb 1901-25 Jan 1902). New York, NY: P. F. Collier and Son, Publishers, 40 cm. weekly. Condition—fragile.

P. 4. *Confederate Veteran*, vol. 7, no. 7; vol. 8, no. 5, 12; vol. 9, no. 6, 12; vol. 13, no. 6; vol. 15, no. 2, 4, 5, 6, 7; vol. 16, no. 2, 3, 4, 6, 7, 9, 11; vol. 17, no. 1, 2, 4, 7, 11, 12; vol. 18, no. 1, 7, 9, 11, 12; vol. 19, no. 1, 3, 4, 5, 8, 9, 11, 12; vol. 20, no. 1, 2, 4—12; vol. 21, no. 1—12; vol. 22, no. 1—12; vol. 23, no. 1—11; vol. 24, no. 1—12; vol. 25, no. 1—12, vol. 26, no. 1, 2, 4—7, 9—12; vol. 28, no. 2, 12; vol. 30, no. 1, 3, 6—8; vol. 31, no. 1—3, 5—7, 9, 12; vol. 32, no. 1—3, 5—7, 9—12; vol. 33, no. 1—12; vol. 34, no. 2—5, 7—10; vol. 35, no. 5, 10—12; vol. 36, no. 1—10, 12; vol. 37, no. 1—10, 12; vol. 38, no. 3—5, 7—11, vol. 39, no. 3—6, 8, 10—12 (July 1899—Dec 1931). Nashville, TN: Trustees of the Confederate Veteran. 27 cm. monthly. Condition.—fragile.

*P. 5. *The Children's New Church Magazine*, vol. 29, no. 5 (Nov 1869). Boston, Mass: O. Clapp. 18¼ cm. monthly. Condition—no cover, water damaged.

*P. 6. *Dunn's Quarterly*, vol. 7, no. 4 (Dec 1893). Chicago, IL: W. P. Dunn Co. 24 cm. quarterly. Condition—no cover, pages clipped, some pencilled annotations.

P. 7. *The East Tennessee Historical Society's Publication*, vol. 33—39, 43, (1961—1967, 1971). Knoxville, TN: East Tennessee Historical Society. 25 cm. annually. Condition—excellent.

P. 8. *Harper's Weekly*, vol. 4, no. 177 (19 May 1860) Cover tearsheet; 22

June 1861; illus. tearsheet; 31 Aug 1861, illus. tearsheet; April 1862, illus. tearsheet; vol. 6, no. 288, cover tearsheet; 11 Oct 1862, illus. tearsheet; 26 Dec 1863, two illus. tearsheets; 10 Sept 1864, illus. tearsheet; 5 May 1866, illus. tearsheet; 16 Feb 1867, illus. tearsheet; vol. 12, no. 593 (9 May 1868); vol. 14, no. 729 (17 Dec 1870); vol. 48, no. 2482 (16 July 1904). New York, NY: Harper and Brothers. 34 cm. weekly. Condition—fragile.

*P. 9. *The Independent*, vol. 70, no. 3262 (11 June 1911). New York, NY:S. W. Benedict. 25 cm. weekly. Condition—no cover, water stained.

P. 10. *Journal of Southern History*, vol. 42, no. 4; vol. 43, no. 2—4 (Nov 1976; May, Nov 1977). New Orleans, LA: Southern Historical Association. 23 cm. quarterly. Condition—excellent.

P. 11. *The Ladies Pearl*, vol. 5, no. 12; vol. 11, no. 4, 11 (Dec 1872; April, Nov 1877). Nashville, TN and St. Louis, MO: n.p. 21, 23 cm. monthly. Condition—no cover, fragile.

*P. 12. *The Ladies Pearl and Electra*, vol. 3, no. 1 (May 1885). Louisville, KY: I. M. Leyburn. 25 cm. monthly. Condition—torn cover, stained, fragile.

P. 13. *The Ladies World*, vol. 21, no. 6; vol. 24, no. 3 (June 1900; March 1903). New York, NY: S. H. Moore & Company. 41 cm. monthly. Condition—fragile, stained.

P. 14. *Leslie's Weekly*, vol. 92, no. 2384 (18 May 1901). 2 copies. New York, NY: Judge Co. 40 cm. weekly. Condition—both fragile, one with stains from scotch tape mending on spine, and both with pages split in half across width from folding.

P. 15. *Meriwether's Weekly* (originally *The Free Trader*), vol. 1, no. 1—vol. 4, no. 82 (3 Dec 1881—11 Aug 1883). Memphis, TN: Avery and M. L. Meriwether. 37 cm. weekly. Condition—bound in two volumes and paper fragile. Annotated throughout by M. L. Meriwether. Very rare. Note M. L. Meriwether's interview with English literary figure Oscar Wilde (17 June 1882). Donated to West Tennessee Historical Society by M. L. Meriwether, St. Louis, MO, in Jan 1949 with extra table of contents and several clippings he donated later filed in front of vol. 1, with copy of letter, 24 Jan 1949 from Marshall Wingfield, President of West Tennessee Historical Society to Frederick Lewis Allen, *Harper's Magazine*, New York, NY, 1 p., outlining history and importance of *Meriwether's Weekly* and suggesting that Harper's use the Oscar Wilde interview; there is no indication of Allen's response.

P. 16. *The Moon*, vol. 1, no. 14, 30 (2 March—23 June 1906). Edited by W. E. B. DuBois. Memphis, TN: E. L. Simon and Company. 29 cm. weekly. Condition—xerox copy, unbound.

P. 17. *Museum Quarterly*, vol. 1, no. 1-3 (Summer 1972 - 1973, Spring). Memphis, TN: Memphis Pink Palace Museum. Publication partially funded by grant from West Tennessee Historical Society. 23 cm. quarterly. Condition—excellent.

P. 18. *The Outlook*, vol. 89, no. 5 (30 May 1908). Outlook Company, New York, NY. 24 cm. weekly. Condition—fragile, stained.

P. 19. *The Ozarks Mountaineer*. vol. 3, no. 6—vol. 5, no. 6 (Feb 1955-April 1957). Branson, MO: Ozarks Commonwealth. 36 cm. monthly, except January. Condition—excellent.

P. 20. *Sunday School Advocate*, vol. 34, no 3, whole no. 785 (14 Nov 1874). New York, NY: Rev. J. H. Vincent. 36 cm. bimonthly. Condition— torn, fragile.

P. 21. *Tennessee Historical Quarterly*, vol. 36, no. 2; vol. 37, no. 1 (Summer 1977, Spring 1978). Nashville, TN: Tennessee Historical Society. 25 cm. quarterly. Condition—excellent.

P. 22. *United Daughters of the Confederacy*, vol. 7, no. 9; vol. 8, no. 1, 2, 4— 12; vol. 9, no. 1, 3—10, 12; vol. 10, no. 1—6, 8—12; vol. 11, no. 1—3, 5, 7, 9—12; vol. 12—27 complete; vol. 23, no. 1—12; vol. 29, no. 1—10, 12; vol. 30, no. 1—12. Richmond, VA: United Daughters of the Confederacy. 30 cm. monthly. Condition—only 1943-1964 bound in paperboards.

P. 23. *The University of Tennessee Record*, vol. 62, no. 3; vol. 64, no. 3 (May 1959; May 1961). Knoxville, TN: University of Tennessee. 23 cm. bimonthly. Condition—excellent.

P. 24. *The Weekly Toiler*, vol. 3, no. 4—vol. 7, no. 29 (20 June 1888—28 June 1892). Nashville, TN: Agricultural Wheel and Farmers' Alliance of Tennessee. 51 cm. weekly. Condition—bound in two volumes; good.

P. 25. *The Western Historical Quarterly*, vol. 1, no. 1—4; vol. 2, no. 1, 3, 4; vol. 3, no. 1—4; vol. 4, no. 1—3; vol. 5, no. 1—3; vol. 6, no. 3—4; vol. 7, no. 1—4; vol. 8, no. 2—4 (Jan 1970—Oct 1977). Logan, Utah: Western History Association. 24 cm. quarterly. Condition—excellent.

5

MAPS
(Provenance Unknown)

Mp 1. Army Service School. Map of Gettysburg and Antietam in 1863. 62 x 58 cm. Black and white on paper with a scale 1:21,120. Ft. Leavenworth, Kansas, 1913.

Mp 2. Harris, Tommy D. "A Literary Map of Tennessee: The Volunteer State." 75 x 56 cm. Three color multilith on paper, with a scale of c. 1:1000. Memphis: Whitehaven High School, 1956.

Mp 3. Johnson, Gordon. Battle of Franklin, TN in 1864. 50 x 54 cm. Blueprint with a scale of 1:5236. Drawn 7 May 1945, Copyright Monroe F. Cockrell, V.M.I., 1907.

Mp 4. Lawrence, William. Map of Memphis. 30 x 22 cm. Xerox copy of black and white on paper, with a scale of 1:10,000. n. l.: n.p., 1819.

Mp 5. Sanger, W. P. S. Plan of the navy yard in the harbor of Memphis, TN in 1844. 63 x 46 cm. Photograph of black and white on paper, with a scale of 1:1620, n.l.: n.p., 1944.

Mp 6. Shiloh National Military Park Commission. Map of Shiloh battlefield in 1862. 71 x 55 cm. Black and white on paper, with a scale of c. 1:1230. n.l.: n.p., 1900.

Mp 7. Palumbo, Frank P., Jr. Official city map of Memphis, TN. 122 x 115 cm. Black and white on paper, with a scale of 1:18,000. Memphis; Memphis Department of Public Works, 1964.

Mp 8. Ring, Emery L. The military campaigns of Nathan Bedford Forrest, 1861-1865. 71 x 71 cm. Black and white on paper, with a scale of 1:887. Copyright Monroe F. Cockrell, V.M.I., 18 September 1941. "Based on Wyeth's life of Forrest."

Mp 9. U. S. War Department. Office of the Chief of Engineers. "Military Maps illustrating the Operations of the Armies of the Potomac and James, May 4, 1864 to April 9, 1865 including Battlefields of the Wilderness, Spottsylvania, Northanna, Totopotomoy, Cold Harbor, the Seige of Petersburg and Richmond, Battlefields of Five Forks, Jetersville and Sailor's Creek, Highbridge, Farmville and Appomattox Court House." 32 sheets. 43 x 60 cm. Three color multilith on paper, with a varying scale. Washington, DC: U. S. War Department, 1869.

Mp 10. Memphis, TN. Map of M. C. Pearch and Willo Williams. Subdivisions of Lot 122, Trigg Tract, being offered for sale at auction, 26-27 April 1888. 53 x 35 cm. Black and white on paper, laminated auction broadside, with unknown scale. Memphis, TN: Whitmore Print, 1888.

Mp 11. Bird's eye view map of City of Memphis, TN, 1870. 46 x 31 cm. Negative photostatic copy of black and white on paper (original in Memphis Room of Memphis and Shelby County Library and Information Center.); scale unknown. n.l.: n.p., 1870.

6
ARTIFACTS

CLOTH:

A 1. Cotton flag, official flag of American Revolution Bicentennial Commission, 1976, 186 x 124 cm. Donated by Tennessee Bicentennial Revolution Commission, Nashville, 1976.

A 2. Acetate flag, official flag of the Tennessee American Revolution Bicentennnial Commission, 1976, 186 x 124 cm. Donated by Tennessee Bicentennial Revolution Commission, Nashville, 1976.

A 3. Four ribbons from reunions of United Confederate Veterans, including two from the 10-13 May 1899 reunion in Charleston, S.C. reunion and two from the Hiram S. Bradford Bivouac Brownsville, TN, n.d. Donated by Alice Lake Morrison, New Johnsonville, TN, 12 June 1969.

A 4. Spanish lace shawl of Ellen Doyle Costıllo, who came to Memphis from Ireland, c. 1832, 294 x 210 x 184 cm. Shawl is of natural llama wool knotted in floral pattern. Separated from Ella Costillo Bennett Manuscripts (see AM 3).

A 5. Black silk jacket of Ellen Doyle Costillo, c. 1836. 36 cm. from shoulder to shoulder; 37 cm. down the back; has some rot under the arms. Separated from Ella Costillo Bennett Manuscripts (see AM 3).

A 6. White lace collar of Ellen Doyle Costillo, mid 19th century. Collar made with scalloped edges in V shape, each side of which is 77 x 55 x 26 cm. Separated from Ella Costillo Bennett Manuscripts (see AM 3).

A 7. White handkerchief with lace borders of Ellen Doyle Costillo, mid 19th century, 34 x 30 cm. The name "Bennett" has been printed in black ink on one corner of the handkerchief. Ella Costillo Bennett carried this handkerchief on a gold ring in Chicago at the Press Club with a black dress decorated by yards of black lace, and perhaps also the lace collar described in above entry (A 6). Separated from Ella Costillo Bennett Manuscripts (see AM 3).

A 8. Cameo pin of women's head mounted on separated black wooden shell background (now broken), belonged to Ellen Doyle Costillo. Worn with jacket (A 5), c. 1836. Separated from Ella Costillo Bennett Manuscripts (see AM 3).

A 9. Doll with painted china head, cloth body, and black dress with white lace collar, black shirt ruffles, left sleeve missing; belonging first to Ella

38

Costillo Bennett and then to child of Confederate officer, 1860's, 31 cm. long. Separated from Ella Costillo Bennett Manuscripts (see AM 3).

A 10. Quilted white silk lined baby bonnet of Ella Costillo Bennett, 1865, 17 x 13.5 cm. Separated from Ella Costillo Bennett Manuscripts (see AM 3).

A 11. Quilted white cotton baby bib, edged in lace with word "BABY" embroidered on it, of Ella Costillo Bennett, 1865, 24 x 17.5 cm. Separated from Ella Costillo Bennett Manuscripts (see AM 3).

A 12. One pair of white leather baby shoes embroidered and edged with lace and tied with string laces, of Ella Costillo Bennett, 1865, 11.5 x 11.5 cm. Separated from Ella Costillo Bennett Manuscripts (see AM 3).

A 13. One pair of white woolen baby mittens stitched with blue thread on glove and woolen ruffle, of Ella Costillo Bennett, 1865, 11 x 6.5 cm. Separated from Ella Costillo Bennett Manuscripts (see AM 3).

A 14. One pair of white silk baby stockings, of Ella Costillo Bennett, 1865, 35 x 9 cm. Separated from Ella Costillo Bennett Manuscripts (see AM 3).

A 15. White baby blouse with lace at sleeve and arms, of Ella Costillo Bennett, 1865, 33 x 18 cm. Separated from Ella Costillo Bennett Manuscripts (see AM 3).

A 16. White silk baby dress, with lace at neck and collar and pale blue and yellow flowers embroidered on skirt, of Ella Costillo Bennett, 1865 945 cm. from neck to skirt hem and 29 cm. at waist. Light stains on skirt. Separated from Ella Costillo Bennett Manuscripts (see AM 3).

A 17. Quited white baby night robe, with lace at neck, two ribbons in front, and embroidery outlining each pattern piece, of Ella Costillo Bennett, 1865, 75 cm. from neck to skirt lace and 16 cm. shoulder to shoulder. Separated from Ella Costillo Bennett Manuscripts (see AM 3).

A 18. Padded crewel embroidery of flowers and a bird on black velvet oval, by Mary L. Costillo at St. Agnes Covent in Memphis, 1874, 26.5 x 25 cm. Separated from Ella Costillo Bennett Manuscripts (see AM 3).

A 19. Triangular piece of red paisley shawl of Ellen Doyle Costillo and her mother Mrs. Doyle, early 19th century, 146 x 105, 96 cm. One edge roughly cut, another fringed, the third woven into selvage. The shawl has one tear and numerous moth holes. Separated from Ella Costillo Bennett Manuscripts (see AM 3).

A 20. Cross-stitched sampler made by Julia Ann Beekman, 1817, 32 x 23 cm. Sampler is badly faded and shows letters, name of seamstress, and picture of house surrounded by a tree and a flower on each side. Beekman's name and capital letters A, E, O, R, and W were stitched in dark thread, which has bled. The sampler is glued to a magazine illustration of a girl holding a candle by Harrison Fisher, 1911, from a 1912 issue of Cosmopolitan magazine. Separated from the Marshall Wingfield Manuscripts (see AM 13).

A 21. Blue acetate velvet cover for historical highway markers, outlined in gold cord and braid. West Tennessee Historical Society, 1960's, 117 x 109 cm. Made for the West Tennessee Historical Society by the Home Economics Department of Memphis State University, and first used at the ceremonies unveiling the Tennessee Historical Commission marker for Memphis State University on Central Avenue in Memphis; later enlarged and used on other markers.

METAL:

A 22. Sword, allegedly of General Edmund Kirby Smith (CSA), c. 1860, 93 cm. in length. Donated by Mrs. Maury T. Reid, Memphis, 21 March 1958. Allegedly, ownership passed from General Smith to Bishop Quintard, who passed it on to Rev. Dr. Arthur Howard Noll of Memphis. Dr. Noll, who may have been Registrar at the University of the South, 1902-1915, passed the sword on to his son Maxwell Noll, who gave it to Mrs. Reid.

A 23. Great Seal of the Confederacy (allegedly the only known facsimile) impressed on white gold, c. 1860, 8.5 cm. in diameter, framed under glass accompanied by a silver and a copper Memphis Sesquicentennial medallion, each 3.5 cm. in diameter. On back of frame is xerox copy of a clipping, 22 Jan 1956, from the *Arkansas Gazette*, giving the alleged history and provenance of the seal. Donated by Marshall Wingfield, Memphis, after 1956.

A 24. Silver Tennessee Bicentennial medal with stand, 1976, 5 cm. in diameter. Donated by Tennessee Bicentennial Commission, Nashville, TN, 1977.

A 25. Two silver forks of Rev. and Mrs. G. A. Klein, late 19th century, 18 cm. long. Rev. and Mrs. Klein, the former Madeline May Miner, received the forks, engraved "Woodlawn", as a wedding present from their neighbors in La Grange, TN, where Rev. Klein was pastor of the Methodist Church. Donated by Elsie May Miner Ballard, Memphis, n.d.

A 26. Hand-forged iron corner brace, bolt, and nut, n.d., removed from Second Presbyterian Church at Main and Beale Streets, Memphis, during its razing. Measurements of the U-shaped bolt with threaded ends are 53.5 cm., of the bolt stamped to fit threaded ends of brace are 36 x 7.5 cm., and of the square nut thread to screw on brace ends is 6 cm. Donated by Charles A. Bobbitt, Memphis, 1974.

A 27. Hollow bronze bust of Marshall Wingfield, 33 cm. tall, mounted on wood block, 17 x 17 x 12 cm., 1955. Donated by the sculptor Betty Jo Godwin, 1955.

METAL AND WOOD:

A 28. Plaque, metal on wood, received by Marshall Wingfield, n.d., as a member of the Salvation Army Advisory Board, 17½ x 13½ cm. Separated from the Marshall Wingfield Manuscripts (see AM 13).

A 29. Plaque, metal on wood, presented to Marshall Wingfield in 1944 by the Memphis Negro Junior Chamber of Commerce as their Community Service Award, 29½ x 24½ cm. Separated from the Marshall Wingfield Manuscripts (see AM 13).

WOOD:

A 30. Wooden plaque with decal, received by Marshall Wingfield as a member of Sertoma, International, n.d., 31 x 21 cm. Separated from the Marshall Wingfield Manuscripts (see AM 13).

A 31. Peg leg of unfinished wood, once thought to belong to early 19th century Tennessee Representative Adam Huntsman; 18 cm. wide with one side piece rising 22 cm. from the leg pad, and the other piece rising 63.5 cm. Provenance unknown.

A 32. Wooden lectern, mid-twentieth century; rising 31 cm. in front and 28½ in back, and being 30.5 cm. in width. Provenance unknown.

PLASTIC:

A 33. Round Seal of the State of Tennessee, plastic, painted to resemble bronze, 1970's, 60.5 cm. in diameter. Donated by Charles A. Bobbitt, Memphis, 1974.

A 34. Square Seal of the City of Memphis, plastic, painted to resemble bronze, 1970's, 60.5 cm. on a side. Donated by Charles A. Bobbitt, Memphis, 1974.

VERTICAL FILE

Items separated from the Marshall Wingfield Manuscripts (see AM 13) are marked with an asterisk. Provenance of items without an asterisk is unknown.

V 1. Anniversary—West Tennessee Historical Society

V 2. Archeological Investigation—Netherland Inn Complex, Kingsport, TN, 1973

*V 3. Army—Handbook, 1940

V 4. "Authors of Tennessee", English Department, Whitehaven High School, Memphis, TN, 1965

*V 5. "John Keith Benton, 1896-1956. Two Tributes", Vanderbilt Divinity School, Nashville, TN, 1956.

*V 6. Bolton High School, Arlington, TN - Evaluation, 1952

V 7. Calendar—Memphis Sesquicentennial, 1968

V 8. Capitols—Tennessee, 1967

V 9. "The Christian Brothers in Memphis, 1871-1971", 1971

*V 10. Churches and the Air Force Manual, 1960

V 11. Churches, Memphis, n.d.

V 12. Churches, Methodist in Arlington, TN, 1956

*V 13. Churches, Presbyterian in West Tennessee, 1940s-1974

V 14. City planning and redevelopment law in South Fulton, TN, 1968

V 15. Community Life, Bemis, TN, 1950s

V 16. Confederacy, 1895, 1954, 1969

V 17. Coppock, Paul R., 1950, 1977

V 18. Creative Historical Writing, 1969

*V 19. Crockett, David, 1955

V 20. Davis, Jefferson, 1890, 1977

*V 21. Dairy—Alexander Means—1861, 1949

V 22. East Tennessee Historical Society, 1969

*V 23. Farm Life, c. 1942

V 24. Fayette County—150 years, 1974

V 25. Flood Control in the Lower Mississippi Valley, 1976

*V 26. Gaston, John, 1941

V 27. Genealogy, c. 1952-1957

V 28. Genealogy—Kentucky Researcher, 1963, 1964

V 29. Genealogy—Tennessee Researcher, 1963

V 30. Haywood County, Sesquicentennial, 1973

*V 31. Health Attitudes, 1932

V 32. Health Department—Memphis - Shelby County - Annual Report, 1968-69

V 33. History—Fiction—America, 1953

V 34. History—Johnson City, TN, c. 1963

V 35. History—Memphis—The Christine School, 1952

V 36. Insurance, 1914

*V 37. Impeachments—TN, 1957

*V 38. Jones, Casey, 1956

*V 39. McMillin, Benton—Speech, Wool on the Free List, 1892

*V 40. "Malone, Walter: His Life and Works", 1916

V 41. Medical Society—Arkansas, 1905

*V 42. Memoirs—Mrs. B. F. Turner, 1952

V 43. Memphis Business, 1957, 1969

V 44. Memphis—A Child's History, 1969

V 45. Memphis—Historical Sketch by Chamber of Commerce, 1947

V 46. Memphis—Sesquicentennial 1819-1969—newspaper supplements, 1969

V 47. Memphis Social Register and Directory, 1935, 1937

V 48. Memphis—Yellow Fever Memorial, n.d.

V 49. Mississippi River (Lower) Channel Improvement, map, 1968

V 50. Missouri—History, 1969

V 51. Museums—TN, 1963, 1966

V 52. Names of places, TN, 1960's

V 53. National banks—United States, 1953, 1964

V 54. Newspaper Carriers, 1950's

V 55. Newspapers—Johnsonville Times

V 56. Newspaper on Microfilm, Tennessee and South, Sales Lists, 1960-1968

V 57. Nursery Rhymes, "Little Bo Peep", c. 1890

*V 58. Paper Industry, 1952

V 59. Poetry, 1936

*V 60. Poetry Society of Tennessee, a history, c. 1969

V 61. Politics and Government, McNairy Co., TN, 1952

V 62. Politics and Government—TN, 1957, 1960, 1963

V 63. Presidents—United States—Election, 1968

*V 64. Public Library—TN, 1953, 1959

V 65. Recreation, 1973

V 66. Religious Literature, 1850's, 1955

V 67. Retirement and Income—Teachers—Carnegie Foundation, 1906

*V 68. Segregation—A Challenge to Democracy, 1950

V 69. Sheriff's Department, Shelby Co., TN, 1959

V 70. Southeastern State—History, 1959

V 71. Tennessee—Southwestern-At-Memphis—Centennial Celebration, 1950

*V 72. Tennessee—Historical Homes, Fayette County, 1974

V 73. Tennessee—History, 1959, n.d.

V 74. Tennessee—Parks

V 75. Tennessee—Pictorial Works, 1863-1872

*V 76. Tennessee State Publications, Lists, 1957-1960

V 77. Trials (Murder), 1958

V 78. United States—History—Civil War, 1954, 1960, n.d.

*V 79. Virginia Law Review—"Dixon-Yates and the Public Interest", 1955

*V 80. Women Poets, 1947, 1973

8
SHEET MUSIC
(Provenance Unknown)

SHEET MUSIC

M 1 *Strauss, Johann*
    "Festival Waltzes," by Johann Strauss. Oliver Ditson & Company Publishers, Boston, 1872.

M 2 *Balfe, M. W.*
    "The Young Nadir," by M. W. Balfe, lyrics by Alfred Bunn. E. Ferrett & Company Publishers, New York.

M 3 "Song of the Enchantress," by M. W. Balfe, lyrics by Alfred Bunn. E. Ferrett & Company Publishers, New York.

M 4 "She Loves Him," by M. W. Balfe, lyrics by Alfred Bunn. E. Ferrett & Company Publishers, New York.

M 5 "Who Has Not Heard O'er Valley and Hill?" by M. W. Balfe, lyrics by Alfred Bunn. E. Ferrett & Company Publishers, New York.

M 6 "The Happy Days of Life are O'er," by M. W. Balfe, lyrics by Alfred Bunn. E. Ferrett & Company Publishers, New York.

M 7 "The Pirates' Chorus," by M. W. Balfe, lyrics by Alfred Bunn. E. Ferrett & Company Publishers, New York.

M 8 *Farmer, Henry*
    "Farmer's Calop," by Henry Farmer. E. A. Benson Publishers, Memphis, 1868.

M 9 *Wade, J. (arr.)*
    "We are Coming Sister Mary," arranged by J. Wade. C. Sheard Publishers, London

M 10 *Hess, Charles*
    "Ah! Woe is Me," by Charles Hess, lyrics by L. Bernard. E. Morton Publishers, Nashville, 1854.

M 11 *Ordway, John P.*
    "Let Me Kiss Him for His Mother," by John P. Ordway. Oliver Ditson & Company Publishers, Boston, 1859.

M 12 *Heller, S.*
    "Spring Morning," by S. Heller. F. A. North & Company Publishers, Philadelphia.

M 13 *Mercadante, S.*
"Ave Maria," by S. Mercadante, adapted by W. Raphaelson. J. L. Peters Publishers, New York, 1871.

M 14 *Fox, Eddie*
"The Watermill," by Eddie Fox, lyrics by D. C. McCallum. Charles F. Fischer Jr. Publishers, Philadelphia, 1877.

M 15 *White, C. A.*
"When The Leaves Begin to Turn," by C. A. White. White, Smith & Company Publishers, Chicago, 1878.

M 16 *Kennedy, H.*
"Little Empty Cradle," by H. Kennedy. London, 18??.

M 17 *McKee, Andy*
"Dancing in the Barn," by Andy McKee, lyrics by Tom Turner. T. B. Harms & Company Publishers, New York, 1878.

M 18 *Florence, Marion*
"Tit-Tat-To Schottische," by Marion Florence, lyrics by J. A. Getze. Lee & Wlker Publishers, Philadelphia, 1860.

M 19 *Hays, Will S.*
"Mollie Darling," by Will S. Hays. J. L. Peters Publishers, New York, 1871.

M 20 *Wilson, G. D.*
"Tripping Thro The Meadows," by G. D. Wilson. White & Goullaud Publishers, Boston, 1871.

M 21 *Forshay, D. E.*
"Dress Parade-Polka Militaire," by D. E. Forshay. H. A. French Publishers, Nashville, 1891.

M 22 *Bellak, J.*
"The Ark of Our Union," by J. Bellak. J. L. Peters & Brothers Publishers, Saint Louis, 1866.

M 23 *Blockley, John*
"My Childhood's Home," by John Blockley, lyrics by Mrs. Norton. Cramer, Addison & Beale Publishers, London, 18??.

M 24 *Eastburn*
"Friendless and Sad," by Eastburn, lyrics by Elmer Ruan Coates. White & Company Publishers, Boston, 1874.

M 25 *FitzGerald, Mrs. Edward*
"The Dying Girl to Her Lover," by Mrs. Edward Fitz Gerald, lyrics by Winthrop M. Praed. Firth & Hall Publishers, New York, 184?.

SHEET MUSIC

M 26 *Gabriel, V.*
"Out In the Streets," by V. Gabriel. G. Andre & Company Publishers, Philadelphia, 18??.

M 27 *Balfe, M. W.*
"Then You'll Remember Me," by M. W. Balfe. The Current Publishing Company, Philadelphia, 1843. 2 copies.

M 28 *Leslie, Ernest*
"Rock Me To Sleep, Mother," by Ernest Leslie, lyrics by Florence Percy. G. D. Russell and Company Publishers, Boston, 1860.

M 29 *Clarke*
"Te Deum," by Clarke. Coventry & Hollier Publishers, London, 18??.

M 30 *Rutledge, John T.*
"Sallie Horner Round The Corner," by John T. Rutledge. E. Witzmann & Company Publishers, Memphis, 1889.

M 31 *Schultze, Charles*
"Home Sweet Home," by Charles Schultze. J. L. Peters Publishers, New York, 1865.

M 32 *Tucker, Henry*
"The Cottage Round the Corner," by Henry Tucker, lyrics by Mrs. M. A. Kidder. Wm. Jennings Demorest Publishers, New York, 1865.

9
TAPE RECORDINGS

T 1. Temple Houston Morrow. Speech, 13 October 1950, at the unveiling of monument to David Crockett, Trenton, TN. Mr. Morrow spoke at the invitation of the Tennessee Historical Commission. 7" reel. 3 3/4 ips. Donated by Marshall Wingfield, Memphis, n.d.

T 2. Judge F. Lloyd Tatum. Speech, 1 October 1977, on "The Life of Sheriff Buford Pusser of McNairy County, TN," followed by discussion. Given at a meeting of the West Tennessee Historical Society in Selmer, TN. Mrs. Helen Pusser and two other relatives of the late Sheriff Pusser were in the audience. 5" reel. 1 3/8 ips.

MEMPHIS BICENTENNIAL COMMISSION

**INVENTORY OF ITEMS DONATED TO
WEST TENNESSEE HISTORICAL SOCIETY, SUMMER 1977**

	Remaining Stock
MBC 1. "The First Two Hundred Years," pamphlet	50
MBC 2. Memphis Bicentennial posters, 43 x 28 cm	60
MBC 3. Memphis Liberty Bell, half share of stock, paper laminated in plastic, 9 x 6½ cm	10,900
MBC 4. Shelby County yellow metal keychain, 7 x 3⅛ cm in plastic box, 11 x 5 x 1½ cm	2,184
MBC 5. Shelby County yellow metal pendant necklaces, 3 x 3 cm on 31 cm chain in plastic box 9 x 6½ x 1½ cm	270
MBC 6. Liberty Bell black metal banks, 17½ x 11 x 11 cm	62

BACK INVENTORY

BOOKS

I 1. Charles W. Crawford, ed. *Cal Alley.* Memphis, TN: Memphis State University Press, 1973. 51 copies with dust jackets.

I 2. James D. Davis. *The History of The City of Memphis.* Memphis, TN: Hite, Crumpton, & Kelly, 1873. Facsimile edition, 1972. 25 copies with dust jackets.

I 3. James Roper. *The Founding of Memphis.* Memphis, TN: Memphis Sesquicentennial, Inc., 1970. 4 copies.

I 4. Samuel Cole Williams. *Beginnings of West Tennessee.* Johnson City, TN: Watauga Press, 1930. 4 copies, unbound.

BROCHURES:

I 5. "History Books on Memphis and West Tennessee." Memphis, TN: West Tennessee Historical Society, 28 Nov 1977. 2½ cu. ft.

I 6. "The West Tennessee Historical Society." Memphis, TN: West Tennessee Historical Society, early 1970's. 2 cu. ft.

I 7. West Tennessee Historical Society Papers:

Issue Number	Year	Copies Remaining
1	1947	69
2	1948	108
3	1949	54
4	1950	36
5	1951	11
6	1952	34
7	1953	74
8	1954	64
9	1955	63
10	1956	143
index, #1—10		
11	1957	98
12	1958	111
13	1959	79
14	1960	92
15	1961	70
16	1962	102
17	1963	89

BACK INVENTORY

Issue Number	Year	Copies Remaining
18	1964	144
19	1965	130
20	1966	123
index, #11—20		
21	1967	116
22	1968	142
23	1969	152
24	1970	234
25	1971	100
26	1972	36
27	1973	90
28	1974	50
29	1975	140
30	1976	298
no index		
31	1977	320

INDEX
List of Abbreviations

All guide entries are numbered sequentially within each category and the letter designation that precedes each number indicates the category of collection. For instance, V 20 is the twentieth item in the Verticle File. The following is a list of abbreviations for the different categories.

A	—	Artifacts
AM	—	Archives and Manuscripts
B	—	Books
I	—	Back Inventory
M	—	Sheet Music
Mp	—	Maps
MBC	—	Memphis Bicentennial Commission
P	—	Periodicals
PH	—	Photographs and Images
T	—	Tape Recordings
V	—	Verticle File

Abelard and Heloise	B7
Abolitionism	AM3, AM9, Ph6
Acceptance and Unveiling of the Statue of Andrew Jackson	B118
Actors	AM10:31, AM10:44
Adamson, C. B.	AM2
After Thoughts, A Sequel to My Yesteryears	B73
Agriculture	AM11, Ph10, Ph24, V23
Agricultural Wheel and Farmer's Alliance of Tennessee	P24
"Ah! Woe is Me"	M10
Alabama	AM10:9, V70
Alderson, William T.	V73
Alexander, Thomas Benjamin	B1
Allison, David	AM10:3
Ambulance Service	AM10:9
America In Our Time, 1896-1946	B30
American Bicentennial Revolution Commission	A1—2, A24, MBC1—6
American Historical Association	B2
American Missionary Association	V68
The American Woman	P1
Anderson, Inez Elliot	V60
The Annals of Tennessee to the End of the Eighteenth Century	B90
Applegate, Mrs. Annie Lee	AM2
Archeology	AM4, V2

"The Ark of Our Union"	M22
Arkansas	P19, P24, V41
Arkansas Gazette	A23
Arkansas Medical Society	V41
Arlington, TN	V6, V12
Army Service School	Mp1
Artifacts	A1—34, MBC3—6
Art Work of Memphis	B107
Association for the Preservation of Tennessee Antiquities	AM8
As They Saw Forrest	B48
Athletics	AM10:46
"Ave Maria"	M13
Avery, Robert Sterling	B43
Bacon, William James	B3
Bailey, E. O.	AM10:45
Baker, Thomas Harrison	B4
Balfe, M. W.	M2—7, M27
Ballard, Elsie May Miner	A25
Banking	V53
Banks	MBC6
Baring-Gould, Sabine	AM10:28
Baron Hirsch Congregation	B96
Barrow, Kate Trader	B5
Barrus, Ben M.	B6
Baughn, Milton L.	B6
Beale Street	AM10:42, B60—61
Beale Street	B60
Beale Street Sundown	B61
Beauvoir, MS	AM10:41
Beecher, Henry Ward	AM3
Beekman, Julia Ann	A20
Beginnings of West Tennessee	B124, I4
Bejach, Louis D.	Ph27
Bellak, J.	M22
Bemis, TN	V15
Bennett, Ella Costillo	A4—19; AM3; B7; P5—6, P12; Ph4—14, Ph22
Bennett, George Sexton	AM3, Ph8
Bennett, Mary Costillo	AM3, Ph10, Ph22
Bennett, Mary L.	AM3, Ph12
Bennett, Raphael Fabian	AM3, Ph11
Bennett, Winnie Lou	AM3, Ph10, Ph22
Benton, John Keith	V5
Bergson, Henri	P9
Bernard, L.	M10
Bible, The	B8
Bible, Jean Patterson	B9
Bibs	A11
Bill of the U.S.A.	B29

The Biography of a River Town	B16
"Black and White"	AM9
Blacks	A29; AM3; P10, P16; V68
Blackwell, Agnes	AM10:4
Blockley, John	M23
Blount, William	B10
The Blount Journal, 1790-1796	B10
Blouse	A15
Bobbitt, Charles A.	A26, A33—34, AM10:25
Bolivar, TN	Ph31
Bolton High School	V6
Bonnets	A10
Boomtowns	AM3
Bowers, Alma Ramsey	AM5, AM10:1, AM10:36—46; Ph1, Ph15, Ph17—18, Ph21, Ph26, Ph37
Boyle, Virginia Frazer	AM10:41, AM10:45; B11
Breihan, Carl W.	B12
Brenan, J. J.	AM10:30
Brockman Family	AM9
Bronze	A27, A33—34
Brooks, Bessie Vance	AM10:39
Brooks, Geraldine	B13
Brooks, Virginia Feild Walton	B14
Brown, John	AM3
Browning, Gordon	Ph27
Brownlow, William G. (Parson)	AM3, Ph6
Brownsville, TN	A3
Bulletin of the Institute of Research	P2
Bunn, Alfred	M2—3, M5—6
Business and Industry	A29; AM3, AM10:11, AM11—12, AM14; P3, P8—9, P12, P15—16, P19; V39, V45, V53—54, V56, V58
Cal Alley	I1
California	AM3, Ph9, Ph12, Ph14, Ph22
Cameo	A8
Cameron, Dr. Alice Woodson	AM12, AM14
The Campaigns of Lieut. Gen. N. B. Forrest	B54
Campbell, Thomas H.	B6
Cannon	AM6, AM10:33
Capers, Gerald Mortimer	B15—16
The Captain and the Submarine CSS H. L. Hunley	B31
Carnegie, Foundation for the Advancement of Teaching	V67
Carroll, Thomas Bradford	Ph38
Carver, George Washington	P10
Cave, Robert Catlett	B17
Cemetaries	AM10:30, AM10:44—45; B70
Centennial Edition, 1840-1940	B19

Chancery Court, Shelby Co., TN	AM9
"A Chapter in the History of Vivum-Ovo"	AM9
Charlotte, TN	AM10:47
Chicago, IL	V16
Children	A9—17; AM3; P1, P5, P11—13; V44, V66
The Children's New Church Magazine	P5
China:	
Boxer Rebellion	P14
Immigrants from	AM3
Chisholm, Hugh J.	V58
Christian Brothers	V9
Christian Church	AM13
Churches	AM10:12, AM10:20
Churches:	
Baptist	V11
Methodist	V11—12
Presbyterian	V11, V13
Civil History of the Government of the Confederate States	B22
Cincinnati Inquirer	Ph8
Citizens Advisory Committee	AM8
The Civil and Political History of the State of Tennessee	B46
Civil Rights	AM9, P16
Civil War	AM2—6, AM8—9, AM10:5—6, AM10:12, AM10:16, AM10:19, AM10:22, AM10:32—34, AM10:36—46, AM10:48, AM12—14, Mp1, Mp3, Mp6, Mp8—9 P4, P8, P15, P17, P22 Ph25—27, Ph29, Ph33, Ph35—37 V16, V20—21, V78
Civil War Centennial	AM13
Clarke	M29
Clarke-Art Engraving Company	Ph35
Clarke, Florence	V31
Clarke, Professor	Ph6
Cleveland, Grover	AM10:42
Cleveland, Mrs. Grover	AM10:42
Clothing	A1—19
Coates, Elmer Ruan	M24
Cobb, Irvin S.	AM10:43
Cochran, Gifford Alexander	B18
Cockrell, Monroe F.	Mp3, Mp8
Collar	A6
Colleges and Universities	A21, AM1, AM10:46, AM10:50, Ph23
Collier's	P3
Colonial Dames of America	AM8
Colorado	AM3, AM16, Ph9—10, Ph22
The Commercial Appeal	AM10:5, B19, V23, V46, V54

INDEX

Confederacy	A3, A23
	AM2, AM5—6, AM9, AM10:1, AM10:4—
	6, AM10:9, AM10:14, AM10:22, AM10:32,
	AM10:34, AM10:36—46, AM10:48
	P4, P8, P15, P17, P22
	Ph13, Ph18, Ph35—37
	V16, V20—21, V78
Confederate Military History	B34
The Confederate Soldier in the Civil War	B56
Confederate Veteran	P4
A Constitutional View of the Late War Between the States	B104
Construction	A26
Conway, Clara	B20
Conyers, Thomas, Sr.	AM10:20
Cooper, Waller Raymond	B21
Coppock, Paul R.	V17
Corlew, Robert E.	B38
Cortese Brothers	P17
Cosmopolitan	A20
Cossitt, Frederick	AM10:39
Costillo, Ellen Doyle	A4—8, A19, Ph5—6
Costillo, Mary L.	A18
Costillo, Michael Charles	Ph6—7
Costillo Family	AM3
"The Cottage Round the Corner"	M32
Cotton	A11; AM11—12, AM14; P10
Cotton Carnival	AM10:36—46
Cotton Picker	AM11
Cowan, Mrs. W. B.	Ph20, Ph33
Cowden, John B.	V77
Coxey's March, 1894	AM3
Cravens, John Park	V27
Crawford, Charles W.	I1
Crockett County, TN	AM10:20
Crockett, David	AM10:3, Ph27, T1, V19
Crump, E. H.	AM10:45
Crump, Mrs. E. H.	AM10:45
Currier, N.	Ph34
Curry, Jabez Lamar Monroe	B22
Daguerrotypes	Ph1
Dames and Daughters of Colonial Days	B13
"Dancing in the Barn"	M17
Davies-Rodgers, Ellen	B23—24, B92
Davis, James D.	B25, I2
Davis, Jefferson	AM9, AM10:14, AM10:34, AM10:39, AM10:
	45,
	B27, B105
	Ph15—16, Ph35,
	V20

Davis, John Henry	B26
Davis, Joseph E.	AM9
Davis Monument	Ph35—36
Davis, Ralph	AM10:40
Davis, Reuben	AM10:33
Davis, Varina Howell (Mrs. Jefferson)	AM9, AM10:39; B27; Ph32; V20
Dear Little Marchioness	B112
Democratic Committee (Memphis)	Ph6
Denton, Eva Tucker	B28
Denver, Colorado	AM3
DeSoto Park (Memphis)	V74
DeWitt, Mrs. J. H.	Ph27
Dick, Elisha Cullen	AM10:15
A Digested Index to the Reported Decisions of the Several Courts of Law in the United States	B122
Directories	V47
Discovering Tennessee	B94
Dix, Dorothy	AM10:45
Dixon-Yates Contract	V79
Doctors	AM3, AM10:9, AM10:15, AM10:41
The Dog Who Came to Dinner	B129
Doll	A9
Donaldson, R. C.	AM4, AM9
Douglas Family	AM9
Douglass, Frederick	AM3
Doyle, Amelia	Ph5
Doyle, Mrs.	A5, A19
"Dress Parade—Polka Militaire"	M21
DuBois, W. E. B.	P16
Duffield, Kenneth Graham	B29
Dumond, Dwight Lowell	B30
Dunbar, Paul Laurence	P16
Duncan, Ruth Henley	B31
Dunlap, F. T.	AM10:48
Dunn's Quarterly	P6
"The Dying Girl to Her Lover"	M25
Each Day a Bonus	B28
Earthquakes	AM3—4
East Tennessee Historical Society	P7, V22
The East Tennessee Historical Society's Publication	P7
Eastburn	M24
Edrington, Mabel Flannigan	B32
Education	A21—22; AM3, AM10:43, AM10:50, Ph19; V4. V6, V9—10, V35, V54, V66—67, V71, V78
Eggleston, George Gary	B33
Eighth Tennessee Volunteers	AM10:32
Elections, presidential	V63

INDEX

Elizabeth II	AM10:45
Elmwood Cemetary	B70
Embroidery	A12—13, A16—18, A20
England	AM10:45
"English Tyranny and Irish Suffering"	AM9
Engravers and Engravings	Ph33—35
Epidemics	AM3, AM10:42: AM14
Europe Now and Then	B74
Evans, Clement Anselm	B34
"Facts the Historians Leave Out"	V78
Fairfax County, VA	AM10:15
Fair, James Rutherford	B35
Farmer, Henry	M8
"Farmer's Calop"	M8
Faulkner, Charles H.	B36
Faulkner, William	AM10:43—44
Fayette County, TN	AM10:8, V24, V72
Federal Writers Project	B37
"Festival Waltzes"	M1
Fighting Tennesseans	B41
First National Bank, Memphis	V53
The First Orgill Century, 1847-1947	B88
"The First Two Hundred Years"	MBC1
Fisher, Harrison	A20
Fisk University	V68
FitzGerald, Mrs. Edward	M25
Fitzhugh, Millsaps	V62
Flags	A1—2, Ph36—37
Flood Control	V49
Florence, Marion	M18
Florida	V70
Flowers, Paul	AM10:37
Folmsbee, Stanley John	B38, P23, V73
Forks	A25
Ford, Jesse Hill	B39
Forest Hill Cemetery	AM10:30
Forrest, Nathan Bedford	AM6, AM9, AM10:16, AM10:19, AM10:33
Forrester, Rebel C.	B40
Forshay, D. E.	M21
Fort Johnsonville Redoubts Trail	V55
The Founding of Memphis	B93, 13
Fox, Eddie	M14
Frances, W. S.	AM10:17
Frances, Mrs. W. S.	AM10:17
Franklin, TN	AM10:2
The Free Trader	AM9, P15
Frey, Herman S.	V20
"The Frogs and I"	V80
"Friendless and Sad"	M24
From Old Mobile to Fort Assumption	B45

Gabriel, V.	M26
Gailor, Thomas	AM10:39, AM10:43—44, Ph17
Gaines, George Towns	B41
Gardner, Alfred	AM10:3
Gardner, Elizabeth McKinne	AM10:5
Gardner, John Almus	AM10:3
Gardner, William Montgomery	AM10:5
Gaston, John	AM10:30, AM10:39, V26
Gaston, Mrs. John	AM10:30
Gates, TN	AM10:20
Genealogy	AM9, AM10:21, AM10:29, AM11—12, AM14, P4, P15, P22, V27—29
George, James Zachariah	AM10:45
Georgia	Ph35, V21, V70
Germantown, TN	AM14
Getze, J. A.	M18
Giers, Carl C.	Ph20
Glory and Tears	B40
Godwin, Betty Jo	A27
Gold	A23
Good Earth Garden Club	AM8
"Good Evening"	AM7
Goodspeed's History of Hamilton, Knox, and Shelby Counties of Tennessee	B42
Goodwyn Institute	AM10:29
Gordon, George W.	AM5, AM10:41; Ph1, Ph18—19, Ph26
Gordon, Mary Hannah (Mrs. George W.)	AM10:41, Ph19
Government	B43, P8, P17; V14, V25, V32, V37, V61—63, V79
Government in Tennessee	B43
Grandeur in Tennessee	B18
Grant, Ulysses S.	Ph33
The Great Book	B23
Greene, Lee Seifert	B43
Greenley, Curran Richard (Mrs. John Wesley Newman)	V59
Greeting Cards	AM3
Griffing, William Brown	B44
Guethe, Arnold	Ph14
Halliburton, Richard	AM10:41
Hamner, James H.	AM6
Hamner, Laura V.	AM6
Hamsley, Bob	V19
Handerchiefs	A7
"The Happiest Days of Life Are O'er"	M6
A Happy House of Life and Other Verses	B5
Harbor (Memphis)	Mp5
Hardeman County, TN	V80
Hardware	A26
Harper's Weekly	P8, Ph15

Harris, John Brice	B45
Harris, Isham	AM10:48
Harrison Washing Machine	Am12
Haynes, Richard	AM10:2
Haynes, Stephen	AM10:2
Hays, Will S.	M19
Haywood, John	B46
Haywood County, TN	V30
Heller, S.	M12
Health and Beauty	AM6; P1, P10—13; V31—32, V41
"Health, Happiness and Success"	V31
Hendrick, Burton Jessee	B47
Henry, Patrick	AM10:43, AM10:48
Henry, Robert Selph	B48
Hess, Charles	M10
Hite, Crumpton and Kelly	I2
Highway Markers	A21, AM10:20, Ph30
Historians	AM1, AM3—4, AM9, AM11, AM13
Historic Madison	B123
Historic Preservation	A26; AM8, AM10:39, AM10:40; AM10:42, AM10:44—45; Ph31—32; V72
"History Books on Memphis and West Tennessee"	I5
History of the City of Memphis	I2
History of the City of Memphis and Shelby County, Tennessee	B55
The History of the Confederate War	B33
History of the Fifty-fifth Field Artillery Brigade	B3
History of Franklin County, Georgia	B59
A History of Houston County	B66
History of Memphis	B25
History of Mississippi County, Arkansas	B32
"History of Tennessee"	V73
Holland, Jean Fox	V80
The Holy Innocents	B24
Home Economics	A21, P1, P11—13
"Home Sweet Home"	M31
Hooker, Ann Frizelle	AM10:21
Hooker, Benjamin	AM10:21
Hooker, Malcolm D.	AM10:21
Horn, Stanley Fitzgerald	B49—50
Houk, Elizabeth Messick	AM10:40
Houston, Sam	AM13
Hubbard, John Milton	B51
Hull, Clifton E.	B52
Huntsman, Adam	A31
Hurlburt, S. A.	AM10:12
Illinois	Ph22, V16
Immigration	AM3

The Independent	P9
"In Hardeman"	V80
Insurance	V36
Inventions	AM11—12
Invisible Empire	B49—50
Invitations	AM10:13
Ireland	A4—5, Ph6—7
Iron	A26
Jacket	A5
Jackson, Andrew	AM10:3, AM10:10, AM10:39; Ph34
Jackson, TN	AM2, V38
Jefferson Davis	B27, B105
Jefferson, Thomas	B53
Jewelry	A8
Johnson City, TN	I4, V34
Johnsonville, TN	V55
Johnson, Gordon	Mp3
Johnson, Marie Sargent Morris (Mrs. Robert)	AM7
Johnson, Robert	AM7
Johnson, Seale	Ph27
Jones, Casey	V38
Jones, Heber W.	AM10:50
Jones, Sam	AM10:44
Jones, Samuel Alroy	AM10:1
Jones, S. W.	Ph20
Jordan, Thomas	B54
Journal of Southern History	P10
Kansas	Mp1
Keating, John McLeod	B55
Kennedy, H.	M16
Kenton: Folklore and Fact	B84
Kentucky	AM9, Ph8, V28, V70
The Kentucky Researcher	V28
Keychain	MBC4
Kidder, Mrs. M. A.	M32
Kingsport, TN	V2
Klein, Mrs. G. A.	A25
Klein, G. A.	A25
Knoxville, TN	P23
Knoxville Whig	Ph6
Ku Klux Klan	AM5, AM9, AM10:41
"The Ku Klux Klan"	AM9
Labor	AM3, P3, P8, P24
Lace	A4—6—7, A9, A11—12, A15—17
The Ladies Pearl	P11
The Ladies Pearl and Electra	P12
The Ladies World	P13
LaBree, Benjamin	B56
LaGrange and Memphis Railroad Company	AM10:17

LaGrange, TN	A25
Lake County, TN	AM4
Lake, Richard P.	Ph25
Lamar, L. Q. C.	AM9
Landgrants	AM10:26, AM10:43, AM10:49
Larson, Melvin Gunnard	B57—58
Lauderdale County From Earliest Times	B86
The Lavonia Times	B59
Lawrence, William	Mp4
Lebanon Methodist Church	AM10:20
Lectern	A32
Lee, George Washington	B60—63
Lee, Robert E.	AM2, AM10:50, Ph21
Lee, Stephen D.	Ph25
Lee, Tom	AM10:45
Leslie, Ernest	M28
Leslie's Weekly	P14
"Let Me Kiss Him For His Mother"	M11
Levytype Company	Ph35
The Liberation of Lord Byron Jones	B39
Liberty Bell	MBC3, MBC6
Libraries	V64
Lieutenant Lee of Beale Street	B114
Life and Labor in the Old South	B87
Lincoln, Abraham	AM10:7, AM10:12
Lincoln, Mary Todd (Mrs. Abraham)	AM3
Lincoln, Robert	AM3
Lineage of the Meriwethers and the Minors From Colonial Times	B80
"Lines on the Back of a Confederate Note"	AM10:1
Literary Memphis	B125
Literature	AM9, AM13
	P1, P3, P5—6, P8—9, P11—16, P18, P20, P22
	V4, V18, V40, V59, V60, V66
Lithography	Ph36
"Little Bo Peep"	V57
"Little Empty Cradle"	M16
Livermore, Mrs. Mary Ashton	B63
Llama wool	A4
Long, N. M.	B64
Louisiana	Ph16, V70
Louisville Courier	Ph8
Lovell, Mansfield	P17
L. Prang and Company	Ph33
Lunan, F. W.	AM10:10
Lyceum Theatre	AM10:31, AM10:44
Lynching	P16
McCain, William David	B65
McCallum, D. C.	M14

McClain, Iris Hopkins	B66
McCorkle, Anna Leigh	B67
McCowat-Mercer Press	V61
McCullough, Margaret C.	V68
McGuffey, William Holmes	B68
McGuffey's Eclectic Reader	B68
McIllwaine, Shields	B69
McKee, Andy	M17
McLean, C. D.	AM10:8
McMillan, Benton	V39
McNairy County, TN	Ph30, T2, V61
Macy, Anne Sullivan	AM10:44
Magevney, Eugene	AM10:39
Magness, Perry Green	V77
Mallory, James	AM10:47
Malone, Walter	AM10:45, V40
Manumission	AM9
"Maple Leaves and Holly"	V59
Marriage	AM14
Marsh, M. A., Family	AM10:35
Mason Depot, TN	AM10:4
Massachusetts	Ph33
The Master of Red Leaf	B71
Mechanization	AM11—12
Medals	A3, A24
Medicine	AM10:4, AM10:9, AM10:15, AM10:34, AM10:41; V41
Melungeons Yesterday and Today	B9
Memoirs of Henry Tillinghast Ireys	B65
Memorial Address on the Life and Character of James Phelan	B116
Memphis	A18, A21—23, A25—26, A29, A34
	AM3, AM5—6, AM8—9, AM10:8, AM10:11—12, AM10:16—18, AM10:23, AM10:25, AM10:27, AM10:29—31, AM10:33, AM10:36—46, AM11—14
	MBC1—6
	Mp2, Mp4—5, Mp7, Mp10—11
	P8, P15—17
	Ph4, Ph6—7, Ph9—10, Ph15, Ph17—18, Ph20, Ph22, Ph25, Ph33, Ph38
Meriwether, Avery	AM9, P15
Meriwether, Elizabeth Avery	AM9, AM10:40, AM10:44; B71—72; P15
Meriwether, Minor Lee (1827-1910)	AM9, B80, P15
Meriwether, Minor Lee (1862-1966)	AM9, AM10:14, AM10:39, AM10:45, AM10:49, AM13; B73—79; P9, P15
Meriwether, Rivers Blythe	AM9
Meriwether Family	AM4, AM9, B80
Meriwether's Weekly	P15
Messages of the Governors of Tennessee	B109

INDEX

Metals	A3, A22—29
Miller, William D.	B81—82
Millsaps, Reuben Webster	AM10:40
Miner, Madeline May	A25
Mining, silver	AM3
Minor, Dabney	AM9
Minor Family	AM9
Mississippi	AM10:4, AM10:19, AM10:33, AM10:42; Ph25, Ph34; V70
Mississippi River	AM3, AM10:44, V25, V49
The Mississippi River: Before and After Mark Twain	B16
Missouri	AM5, AM9, Ph5, Ph22, V50
Mr. Crump of Memphis	B82
Mitchell, Enoch L.	B38, V73
Mittens	A13
Model Railroaders	AM8
"Mollie Darling"	M19
Money	AM10:1, AM10:32, AM10:48
Monuments	Ph35—36
Moody, William Lewis, Jr.	AM10:45
The Moon	P16
Moore, John Trotwood	B83
Moore, Mrs. John Trotwood	V65
More Yesteryears	B75
Morgan, Perry Franklin	AM10:32
Morris, Jno. B.	AM2
Morrison, Alice Lake	A3
Morrison, John	V19
Morrow, John J., Jr.	AM10:9
Morrow, Temple Houston	Ph27, T1
Morton, Dorothy Rich	V72
Moses, G.	Ph16
Mud 'n' Mercy in Memphis	B57
Murder	AM10:7, AM10:34, V77
Murray, Sara Conyers	AM10:20
Museums	AM1, P17, V38, V44, V51
Museum Quarterly	P17
Music	AM10:28; M1—32; P6, P17, V16
"My Childhood's Home"	M23
My First 98 Years	B76
My First 100 Years	B77
My Story of the War	B63
My Yesteryears	B78
Nashville	A1—2; AM10:7; P4, P11, P21; Ph20; V5,
Nashville Union	V8
Nathan Redford Forrest Tennessee State Park	V55, V73
National Bank of Commerce (Memphis)	V53
National Suffragists Convention	AM9

Navy Yard (Memphis)	Mp5
Nazis	AM10:44
Necklaces	MBC5
New Deal	AM9
New Lyceum Theatre	AM10:31
Newman, John Wesley	V59
Newman, Mrs. John Wesley	V59
News, World and United States	P3, P8—9, P11—12, P14—16, P18
Nichols Family	AM3
Nichols, Mary L.	AM3
Night Riders of Reelfoot Lake	B120
"Nineteenth Century Homes of Fayette County"	V72
Nobel Prize for Literature	AM10:43—44
Noll, Arthur Howard	A22
Noll, Maxwell	A22
The North Arkansas Line	B35
North Carolina	V70
Norton, Doretha O.	B84
Norway	AM10:44
Notes of a Private	B51
Nullification and Secession in the United States	B89
Nursery Rhymes	V57
Nurses	AM10:4, AM10:9
Obituaries	AM10:36—46
Official Records of the Union and Confederate Navies in the War of the Rebellion	B117
Ohio	AM10:21, Ph8
"Old Purdy"	V61
Old Stagecoach Inn	Ph30
The Old Stone Fort	B36
An Old Virginia Court	B126
154th Senior Regiment Tennessee Volunteers	AM10:32
One Hundred Years of the Commercial Appeal	B108
"On the Resurrection Morning"	AM10:28
"Onward, Christian Soldiers"	AM10:28
Ordinance	AM6, AM10:33
Ordway, John P.	M11
Oregon	Ph11
Orgill, William	AM10:40, B88
The Other Side	B11
"Out in the Streets"	M26
The Outlook	P18
Overton Park Zoo (Memphis)	AM10:42
Oxford Paper Company (Portland, Maine)	V58

The Ozarks Mountaineer	P19
Paine, Rowlett	AM10:45
Painters and Painting	Ph1, Ph4, Ph6—7, Ph13, Ph37—38
Pate, J. D.	Ph27
Palumbo, Frank P., Jr.	Mp7
Paper Manufacture	V58
Parks	AM10:42, V55, V65, V73—74
Patents	AM11—12
Patton, George	AM10:3
Peg leg	A31
Pennsylvania	Ph35
A People Called Cumberland Presbyterians	B6
Pepper, John Robertson	B85
Percy, Florence	M28
Person, George W.	AM10:45
Peters, George B.	AM10:34
Peters, Mrs. George B.	AM10:34
Peters, Kate Johnson	B86
Phillips, Ulrich Bonnell	B87
Philosopy	P9
Photographers	Ph15—16, Ph18, Ph20
Pickett, Mrs. A. B.	AM10:43
Pictorial Material	A1—34; AM3, AM10:10, AM10:25, AM10:36—46; Ph1—38; V73, V75
Picturesque America	V75
Pilgrimages	AM10:42—43
"The Pirates Chorus"	M7
Placenames	V52
Plaques	A28—30
Planning	AM8, V14, V49, V55, V73
"Plant to Prosper"	V23
Plastic	A33—34
Poe, Edgar Allen	AM9
Poems by William Brown Griffing	B44
Poetry	AM10:1, AM10:6, AM10:23, AM10:28, AM10:35, AM10:41, AM10:43, AM10:45; V59—60, V80
Poetry Society of Tennessee	V60
Police	V69, T2
Politics and Politicians	A31, AM9, P8, P10, P15, P18—19
Polk, James K.	V27
Polyclinic Medical School and Hospital (New York, NY)	AM10:9
Porteous, Clark	B88
Porter, A. R.	AM10:41
Postal Service	AM10:45, P17
Postcards	Ph31—32
Powell, Edward Payson	B89
Praed, Winthrop M.	M25

Preservation	see historic preservation
Price, Samuel W.	Ph33
Priddy, M. C.	AM10:11
Prisons	AM10:45
Prosthetic Devices	A31
Public Welfare	AM10:2, AM10:4, AM10:9, AM10:14
Publishing and Journalism	A7
	AM2, AM4, AM7—9, AM10:5, AM10:18, AM10:24, AM10:36—46
	I1—7
	MBC1—2
	Mp2, Mp7, Mp10
	V31, V46, V54, V56, V58—59, V61, V68, V73, V76—77
Purdy, TN	Ph30
Pusser, Buford	T2
Pusser, Helen	T2
Quantrill and his Civil War Guerrillas	B12
Quilting	A10—11, A17
Quintard, Bishop	A22
Racing	AM10:25, Ph6
Railroads	AM8, AM10:17
Raleigh, TN	V16
Ramsey, E. B.	AM10:39
Ramsey, E. B., Family	AM10:36—46
Ramsey, James Gettys McGready	B90
Randolph, TN	AM10:40
Raphaelson, W.	M13
Rayner, Juan	AM10:16
Real Estate	AM10:45, AM12
Rebel Coach	B121
Recollections of 92 Years	AM9, B72
Reconstruction	AM3, AM9, AM10:42, AM14, P8, P10
Recreation and Leisure	P3, P19
Religion	AM3, AM10:36—46, AM13
	P5—6, P11, P20
	V5, V9—13, V21, V66
Republican Party	V62
Revolutionary War	AM10:2, AM10:20
Ribbons	A3, A17, Ph6
Richardson, R. P.	AM10:5
Richmond, VA	AM2
Ring, Emery L.	Mp8
Riots	AM10:27
River George	B62
Roark, Eldon	B91
Robe, night	A17
Robison, Dan M.	Ph27
"Rock Me to Sleep, Mother"	M28
Rodgers, Ellen Davies	B24—25, B93
Rollins, Bertie Shaw	AM10:47

The Romance of the Episcopal Church in West Tennessee	B93
Roper, James	B93, I3
Rossville, TN	AM10:8
Rothrock, Mary Utopia	B94
Russell, Lillian	AM10:44
Rust, John D.	AM10:38, AM11, AM13
Rust Family	AM11, AM13
Rutledge, John T.	M30
Saint, John C.	AM12, Ph23
St. Agnes Convent (Memphis)	A18, AM3
Saint Family	AM12, AM14
St. Mary's Cathedral, 1858—1958	B26
"Sallie Horner Round the Corner"	M30
Salvation Army Advisory Board	A28
San Francisco, CA, Earthquake	AM3
Sanger, W. P. S.	Mp5
Scates, Elias Erwin	B95
A School History of Tennessee	B95
Scholtz, Belle Kenney	Ph27
Schultze, Charles	M31
Screed of Safari Tribe	B14
Sculptors and Sculpting	A27, Ph27
Seals	A23, A33—34
Second Presbyterian Church, Memphis	A26, AM10:12
Segregation	V68
Selmer, TN	T2
Semmes, Raphael	Ph11, Ph13
Sermons and Addresses	B64
Sertoma International	A30
Sesquicentennials	A23, V7, V30, V46
Shawl, paisley	A19
Shankman, Samuel	B96
Shelby County, TN	AM4—5, AM8—9, AM10:8, AM10:17, AM12, AM13—14
	I1—7
	MBC1—6
	V66
Shelby County Historical Commission	AM8
"She Loves Him"	M4
Sherman, William T.	AM10:12, Ph33
Shiloh National Military Park Commission	Mp6
Shiloh National Military Park	Ph27, Ph29
Shoemaker, Jno.	AM10:13
Shoes	A12
Shortline Railroads of Arkansas	B52
The Shrine in a Temple	B127
Sign On: The First 50 Years of WREC Radio	B97
Silk	A5, A14, A16

Silver	A23—25, AM3
Silver-lined Days	B20
Simms, William Gilmore	B98
Simons, Algie Martin	B99
Simpson, Rubye Tennyson	V80
Skid Row Stopgap	B58
Slaves and Slavery	AM3, AM6, AM9, AM10:3, AM12, P10
Slidell, John	Ph33
Smith, Edmund Kirby	A22
Smith, Gipsy, Jr.	AM10:39
Smith, John	AM10:47
Smyth, Mary Jane	Ph24
Social Forces in American History	B99
Society	V47
Society functions	AM10:36—46
Soldiers	AM10:1—2, AM10:4—6, AM10:9, AM10:12, AM10:16, AM10:19—20, AM10:22—23, AM10:27—28, AM10:32—34, AM10:41—44, AM10:46, AM10:50, Ph2
Somerville, TN	AM10:50, V13
"Song of the Enchantress"	M3
Sons of Confederate Veterans	AM8
Sorrels, William Wright	B100
The South in the Building of the Nation	B101
South Carolina	A3, V70
South Fulton, TN	V14
Southern Bell Telephone and Telegraph Company	V70
The Southerner	B103
Southern Historical Society	B102
Southern Historical Society Papers	B102
Southern Railroad Company	AM8
Southwestern-at-Memphis, 1848-1948	B21
Southwestern-at-Memphis	V71
"Spring Morning"	M12
Stacy, Mrs. C. M.	AM6
Stamps	AM10:11
Standard History of Memphis, Tennessee	B128
Statesmen of the Lost Cause	B47
Stephens, Alexander Hamilton	B104
Stephens, Jack	AM2
Stewart County, TN	AM10:47
Stockings	A14
Stores	Ph3
The Story of Craighead County	B106
"The Straight Gate"	V66
Strauss, Johann	M1
Street Cars	AM10:44
Strode, Hudson	B105
Stubblefield, Mrs. Doyle	Ph34

Stuck, Charles Albert	B106
Suffragism	AM9
Sunday, Billy	AM10:39
Sunday School Advocate	P20
Supreme Court of Errors and Appeals, TN	AM10:47
Swords	A22
Tait, John Leisk	B107
Tales of Old Whitehaven	B67
"Tales of a River Town"	V44
Talley, Robert	B108
Tatum, F. Lloyd	T2
Taylor, Zachary	AM10:10
Tazewell, TN	Ph26
Teachers	V67
"Te Deum"	M29
Tennessee	B37—38
Tennessee:	
General	A24, A33; AM1—15, AM10:32, AM10:48; M2; P8; V37, V51—52, V60, V63—64, V70, V73, V75—76, V78—79
East	A1—2; I4; P7; Ph20; V2, V19, V22, V33—34, V62
Middle	A1—2; AM10:2, AM10:7, AM10:26, AM10:47; M4—5, M7; P4, P11, Ph4, Ph6—7, Ph9—10; V5, V8, V27, V64, V68, V77
West	A3, A18, A21—23, A25—26, A29, A31, A34
	AM1—9, AM10:3, AM10:5, AM10:8, AM10:11—12, AM10:16—20, AM10:23, AM10:26—27, AM10:29—33, AM10:35—46, AM10:50, AM11—13
	I1—7
	MBC1—6
	Mp4—5, Mp7, Mp10—11
	P15—17
	Ph4, Ph6—7, Ph9—10, Ph15, Ph17—18, Ph23, Ph25, Ph29—31
	T1 2
	V1, V4—7, V9—17, V23—26, V29—32, V35—36, V40, V42—49, V53—55, V59, V61—62, V64, V69, V71—72, V74, V80
Tennessee Association of Museums	V51
Tennessee Commission Book, 1796-1801	B110
Tennessee Council of Churches	AM13
Tennessee Historical Commission	A21, Ph30, T1, V2, V18, V63, V76
Tennessee Historical Quarterly	P21
Tennessee Historical Society	P21
The Tennessee Researcher	V29
"Tennessee's Celebrated Case"	V77

Tennessee State Federation of Women's Clubs	B111
Tennessee State Library and Archives	V63, V76
Tennessee Valley Authority	V79
Tennessee, The Volunteer State	B83
Texas	Ph27
Theatre	AM10:31, AM10:44
"Then You'll Remember Me"	M27
Thomas A. R. Nelson of East Tennessee	B1
Tilley, John S.	V78
Time	AM10:45
Tintypes	Ph2—5
Tipps, Charles	Ph27
Tipton County, TN	AM10:4
Tiptonville, TN	AM4
"Tit-Tat-To Schottische"	M18
Todd, D. H.	AM10:6
T. O. Fuller Tennessee State Park	AM4
Tourism	V43, V45, V65
Tracy, A.	B112
Travel	AM3, AM9, AM10:41, AM10:44; P3, P8, P14—15, P19
Trenton, TN	Ph27, T1
Trinity United Methodist Church, Memphis	B113
"Tripping Thro the Meadows"	M20
Tucker, David M.	B114
Tucker, Henry	M32
Tupelo, MS	AM10:44
Turner, Mrs. B. F.	V42
Turner, Tom	M17
Twain, Mark	AM10:39
Twenty-first Louisiana Volunteers	AM10:6
Union County, Indiana	AM10:2
United Confederate Veterans	A3, AM5, AM10:23, Ph25
United Daughters of the Confederacy	P22, V16
United Sons of Confederate Veterans	AM9, AM10:41
University of the South	A22
University of Tennessee	P23
The University of Tennessee Record	P23
U.S. Air Force	V10
U.S. Army	V3, V25, V48, V65
U.S. Army Corps of Engineers	V25, V48
U.S. Bureau of American Ethnology	B115
U.S. Congress	B116, B118
U.S. Council of Churches	AM13
U.S. Internal Revenue Service	AM10:10—11
U.S. Naval War Records Office	B117
U.S. War Department	B119, Mp9
Utley, Buford C.	AM1

Vanderwood, Paul J.	B120
Van Dorn, Earl	AM10:4, AM10:34
Van Dorn-Peters Affair	AM10:34
Vaught, John	B121
Vawter, Mrs. W. M.	Ph36
Velvet	A18, A21
Vespucci, Amerigo	AM10:40
Veterans	AM10:1—2, AM10:5, AM10:9, AM10:20, AM10:23, AM10:27, AM10:33, AM10:41—44, AM10:50
Virginia	AM9, AM10:50
Wade, J.	M9
The War Diary of a Diplomat	B79
War Poetry of the South	B98
The War of the Rebellion	B119
Washing machine	AM12
Washington, George	AM10:15
Watercolors	Ph37
"The Watermill"	M14
Watkins, Thomas R.	AM10:40
Watauga Press	I4
Weakley County, TN	AM10:3
"We are Coming, Sister Mary"	M9
The Weekly Toiler	P24
Well-nigh 50 Years at the Superintendent's Desk	B85
West Point, MS	AM6
West Tennessee Historical Society, Inc.	AM1, AM8, AM21, I5—6, Ph27; T2; V1, V16, V61
West Tennessee Historical Society Papers	AM1, I7
West Tennessee State Teachers College	AM10:46
The Western Historical Quarterly	P25
Wharton, Thomas Isaac	B122
"When the Leaves Begin to Turn"	M15
White, C. A.	M15
Whitehaven High School	Mp2
White House	AM10:13
White, Robert H.	B109, V73
Whitmore Print	Mp10
"Who Has Not Heard O'er Valley and Hill?"	M5
Wilde, Oscar	P15
Wilder, Corporal	Ph26
Williams, Emma Inman	B123
Williams, Samuel Cole	B124, I4
Wills	AM10:15
Wilson, G. D.	M20
Wingfield, Marshall	A20, A23, A27—30 AM1, AM9, AM10:4, AM10:6, AM10:9, AM10:26—27, AM10:31—32, AM10:40,

Wingfield, Marshall—Continued	AM10:45, AM13 B125—127 P15 Ph2, Ph27, Ph29—30 V3, V5—6, V10, V13, V19, V21, V23, V26, V31, V37—40, V42, V58, V60, V64, V68, V72, V76, V79—80
Winston, Geddes	AM10:49
Women	AM3—4, AM6, AM9, AM10:4—5, AM10:9, AM10:20—21, AM10:30—31, AM10:34—46, AM14 P1, P3, P10—15 V80

Beverly Tykes - 1004 Grassland Lane
Nashville, Tenn. 37220
(615) 297-9094